Advance Praise for *The*

"Finally, in a world full of messages about ....q.... .. ..er to achieve success, Michelle Lederman teaches us that *we already have* everything we need to connect with others. A must-read for anyone interested in how to effectively leverage your network . . . by just being yourself."
—Tiffany Dufu, President, The White House Project

"WOW, I simply love this book. I couldn't put it down once I started it. Lederman's insights, gems, and nuggets of brilliance are a must-read for all those climbing the ladder of success in business and life. Seldom does a book say it better or more powerfully regarding the power and importance of the relationships in our lives and give us the roadmap for establishing lifelong friendships. Thank you Michelle for giving us this important and timely gem."
—George C. Fraser, author, *CLICK: Ten Truths for Building Extraordinary Relationships*

"'Likability' is a powerful and often considered intangible component of influence. Michelle Lederman shows that it can be broken down and studied. There are implications here for organizations as well as individuals."
—Irv Schenkler, Clinical Professor of Management Communication; Director, Management Communication Program, Stern School of Business, New York University

"Engaging, insightful and so useful, *The 11 Laws of Likability* is a must-read for working moms looking to expand their networks and cultivate new allies. And let's face it, who wouldn't benefit from some pointers about the best ways to start new conversations? Michelle Lederman's step-by-step approach starts with preparation before the conversation takes place, takes you through the conversation, and then provides guidance on the relationship-building that can take place afterward. Hers is a no-fail approach."
—Suzanne Riss, Editor-in-Chief, *Working Mother* magazine

"A number of components of a complete education are not covered in traditional business school classes. The most successful graduates are those who have learned the art of Networking. The basics of that art are clearly and intelligently stated in these pages. This book is more than a guide to business networking; it can easily serve as a guide to success in both work and life."
—Joan DeSalvatore, CEO, College Bound Advising Today; formerly Assistant Dean, Columbia Business School and Associate Dean, Lehigh University, College of Business and Economics

"Run, don't stroll, to get this book! Michelle Tillis Lederman provides brilliant insights on how to build and maintain meaningful professional relationships—from contact to connection."
—Ann Demarais, co-author, *First Impressions: What You Don't Know About How Others See You*

"The majority of our professional lives revolve around relationships: with clients, bosses, colleagues, etc. Michelle Lederman gives a framework of self-reflection that helps drill down and illuminates that most powerful tool we bring to the table: our authentic self. She shows how we already have what we need—we just need to recognize it."

—Sharon Gala, investments portfolio manager; President 2010–2011, MetLife Women's Investment Network

"The idea of starting from 'the outside in' is critically important—particularly for women and newcomers to the workplace. Michelle's approach was fresh. The anecdotes and use of humor made the book user friendly, and I would recommend it for your home *and* office libraries, as the theories apply in both contexts."

—LaChonne Walton, Director, Human Resources & Administration, Jazz at Lincoln Center

"This is an insightful and practical book. At first I thought, 'I know some people who need to read this!' Then, as I read more deeply, I said, 'Wow, I'm glad *I'm* reading this!' If you believe personality and relationship are important in your business and interpersonal connections, you need to read *The 11 Laws of Likability.*"

—Becky Sheetz-Runkle, author, *Sun Tzu for Women: The Art of War for Winning in Business*

"*The 11 Laws of Likability* offers a fresh, insightful, and readable new perspective on networking. Its focus on connection and relationship building provides a welcome alternative to the 'working a room' approach to networking—and readers will certainly relate to the real-life examples included throughout every chapter. There is no question that this is a book I will refer to often and recommend to those who are looking for practical advice on how to build lasting business relationships."

—Sheryl Parker, Founder, Powwow: A Network for Women Making a Difference

"Michelle Tillis Lederman takes a sustainability approach to relationships. She shows readers how to establish a foundation to build upon and turn a conversation into a connection. This book is practical, tactical, and applicable to those at all conversational skill and professional levels."

—Debra Fine, keynote speaker, trainer, and bestselling author of *The Fine Art of the Big Talk: How to Win Clients, Deliver Great Presentations, and Solve Conflicts at Work*

The 11 Laws
of Likability

The 11 Laws of Likability

■

Relationship Networking . . .
Because People Do Business
with People They Like

Michelle Tillis Lederman

WITHDRAWN

▲AMACOM

American Management Association
New York • Atlanta • Brussels • Chicago • Mexico City • San Francisco
Shanghai • Tokyo • Toronto • Washington, D.C.

Bulk discounts available. For details visit:
www.amacombooks.org/go/specialsales
Or contact special sales:
Phone: 800-250-5308
E-mail: specialsls@amanet.org
View all the AMACOM titles at: www.amacombooks.org

Library of Congress Cataloging-in-Publication Data
Lederman, Michelle Tillis, 1971–
   The 11 laws of likability : relationship networking— because people do business with people they like / Michelle Tillis Lederman.
     p.   cm.
   Includes bibliographical references and index.
   ISBN-13: 978-0-8144-1637-2 (pbk. : alk. paper)
   ISBN-10: 0-8144-1637-3 (pbk. : alk. paper)
   1. Business networks—Psychological aspects.   2. Social networks—Psychological aspects.
3. Interpersonal relations.   I. Title.   II. Title: Eleven laws of likability.
HD69.S8L44   2012
650.1'3—dc23
                                                                                    2011017500

About AMA

American Management Association (www.amanet.org) is a world leader in talent development, advancing the skills of individuals to drive business success. Our mission is to support the goals of individuals and organizations through a complete range of products and services, including classroom and virtual seminars, webcasts, webinars, podcasts, conferences, corporate and government solutions, business books, and research. AMA's approach to improving performance combines experiential learning—learning through doing—with opportunities for ongoing professional growth at every step of one's career journey.

Printing number

10 9 8 7 6 5 4 3 2

For my family,
Michael, James, and Noah
my heart, my smile, my world

Contents

PART C. *After the Conversation: Build Relationships*

Acknowledgments

The first person I must thank is my husband, Michael. Without you, there would be no book. I thank you for your constant feedback, insights, and faith. I thank you for being my sounding board, my greatest supporter, and my best friend. I love you. To my boys, James and Noah, thank you for letting Mommy write, and for the frequent interruptions that gave me much needed breaks. I thank my mother, my father, and my sister, April, for all the lessons you have taught me—those that are in the book and so many that are not.

A special thanks to Ann Demarais for all your support. You have been so giving of your knowledge, your time, and yourself every step of the way through this process. Your experience, perspectives, and guidance were invaluable. I thank my agent, John Willig, for your belief in the project and for not just knowing but explaining to me the nuances of the process.

There are so many people who have helped shape this book. Dave Conti helped me think through the book's structure and content. Lesley Alderman's insights, additions, and feedback brought clarity during the writing process. To my editor, Meeghan Truelove, my heartfelt thanks. You took my words and helped them come to life. You have the greatest energy—it's contagious.

To those who read drafts and gave me feedback—Ann Demarais, Dean Rubino, and Michael Lederman—your comments were thought-provoking and truly appreciated. Rebecca Rodskog and Abby Katoni, I thank you for your constant support throughout the process. I must acknowledge Amy Blumkin, who was an inspiration to me early on in my career and continues to be one to this day.

I thank all the people whose stories are in the book, those whose names are real and those whose names I have changed. All of you have been a source of inspiration and learning.

Many people asked how I chose AMACOM. Although there were many reasons, the first was that I liked the editor, Ellen Kadin. I thank you, Ellen, for your support, patience, and especially your fun spirit.

The **11** Laws
of Likability

Introduction

I used to believe I knew most of what there was to know about connecting with people and building relationships. But one day my belief got completely upended. It happened while I was teaching one of my classes at New York University. The course was about organizational communication, and it was for business school sophomores. The students were there to learn strategic tactics for communicating effectively. Even though we covered a wide range of topics during the semester—from understanding the audience to constructing oral and written presentations—my overarching message was always the same: You must have a purpose for every communication. If you haven't established your intent, I told my students, you are wasting your time and your listener's patience. I pounded home that message at every opportunity.

Then one day I asked my class, "What do you think my objective is this semester? What is my intent?" A young man sitting in the front row eagerly raised his hand. With a big smile he said, "You want us to like you!"

I was startled by his comment, and my answer was swift and seemingly nonchalant. "No, that's not my intent," I scoffed. "I don't really care whether you like me or not." Reflecting on the incident later, though, I realized that my response had been a smokescreen. I did want them to like me; of course I wanted to be liked. Who doesn't?

What bothered me the most was that my response to the student's comment had been so harsh and abrupt, and it was because I was uncomfortable with the accuracy of his assessment. Even if I was willing to admit that I wanted to be liked, of course I didn't want my class to know it. In my mind, someone who wanted to be liked was needy and weak and wasn't very likable.

To this day I'm not sure if the student's comment was intended to be smart-alecky or sincere, but regardless, it had a profound impact on me. It got me thinking about likability, and not just why we want to be liked but why we should want to be liked. That classroom incident changed the course of my work, my approach to teaching and coaching, and my own methods of networking and relationship building. Now I focus on the importance of likability—being likable, liking ourselves, and in turn, liking the people we meet.

Many networking experts urge people to be strategic and deliberate to a fault, focusing on how to work a room and get in front of key people. The act of meeting people and seeking connections begins to feel like a dreaded chore, and when it feels like something you have to do rather than *want* to do, it's hard to motivate yourself to do it at all, let alone do it well.

Contrary to what many networking experts counsel (and what I, too, used to believe), every interaction does not need to have an intent or a specific objective. We do not need to focus with laserlike precision on what our takeaway from a conversation will be, because building relationships is not about transactions—it's about connections. It is about creating opportunities for honest and authentic interactions, and making them advantageous for all parties involved. It's about liking and being liked.

Tapping into likability doesn't mean making everything all perky and bright and constantly being happy. In some ways it's just the opposite. Harnessing likability is about uncovering what is authentically likable—in you, in the other person, in your connection. It is through the strength of what is genuine that meaningful connections build into relationships. The term *networking* is simply another way to think about how to start a relationship. Our relationships are our network. Whether they stem from business or personal situations, our relationships are what support us, connect us, and allow us to progress in all aspects of our lives.

To fully engage the power of likability, we need to understand what it is and how it works. We are all, obviously, different, and that's a fact to be celebrated and embraced. What makes each of us likable is distinct to us. But the basic drivers of likability are the same for us all. I call them the *11 laws of likability*. This book takes an in-depth look at each of these "laws," breaking them down to find out how they function in both business and social settings, and how to fully incorporate them into our lives.

This new likability-based paradigm for networking and building relationships minimizes moments of inauthenticity and missed opportunities. Instead, I'll show you how to uncover what is inherently likable about yourself, and how to share those qualities with the people you meet to create relationships that are honest and real, and that lead to win-win situations for everyone involved. By approaching your interactions through the lens of likability, you can expect to be happier, more comfortable, and more successful in establishing meaningful relationships.

Even those of you who are comfortable approaching new people, generating a conversation, or asking for what you want will benefit from shifting your traditional thinking about how to make connections. Expanding your perspectives on networking and embracing the tenets of likability can open up whole new paths to connecting with people and nurturing strong relationships.

Building fruitful and lasting relationships starts with abandoning the conventional "me"-based thoughts that are so prevalent in the business world and so easy to slip into in our personal lives. "What can this person do for me?" becomes "What can I do for this person?" Likewise, "What can I get out of this situation?" becomes "How does this situation benefit us all?"

You must shift your thinking:

- From Me to Them
- From Work to Any Topic
- From Now to Long Term

Because here is the essential truth about meaningful connections: *It's not about you—it's about the relationship.*

Part A

∎

Before the Conversation: Get Real

My dad always used to say to me and my sister, "The world is a mirror." As a kid, I would repeat the phrase, but I never really thought about what he was trying to tell us. Then one day he stood me in front of a mirror and said, "Smile." I did, and the person in the mirror smiled back at me. He said, "Look angry." I gave the girl in the mirror a nasty look and got the same nasty look right back. He then sat me down and explained the lesson: What you show the world is what the world will show you. The energy you put out, the thoughts you share, are the energy that you will receive from the world, the thoughts you will hear. So true is this that I later realized there are a million sayings that express the same idea: "What you give is what you get," "You reap what you sow," "What goes around, comes around," and my favorite, "Karma's a bitch."

Over the years this concept has crystallized for me. As I completed my education and began building my career, I saw more than ever how "the world is a mirror" plays itself out in life. I noticed that, whether I was working with a new client or an established colleague, the energy I brought to the situation deeply impacted it. If I was having a rough day, the encounter would be difficult. If I was feeling confident and on top of my game, the encounter would be positive and productive. My attitude at any given moment—how I thought, my assumptions about a situation, how I acted—influenced other people's first impressions of me. It was how they formed their perceptions of me, and it influenced the connection between us. The more aware I became of my own mood, the more I was able to ensure that my authentic self came through during different situations, and I was able to adjust my behavior when necessary to communicate in the most effective ways.

What does it all boil down to? Some of the work of making meaningful connections and growing relationships happens before you even meet someone. Taken together, the four chapters in this section are about increasing our awareness of what is genuine and valuable—in short, *likable*—about us, and discovering how the energy we bring to a situation impacts other people's perceptions of us and our ability to connect at a meaningful level. Understanding these things is the first step toward expressing our likability to others. Once we fully recognize this likability, we can harness it to create lasting, mutually positive connections with the people in our lives, whether we've known them for years or are just meeting them for the first time.

1

The Law of Authenticity

"Be your authentic self. Your authentic self is who you are when you have no fear of judgment or before the world starts pushing you around and telling you who you're supposed to be."

—Dr. Phil McGraw (aka "Dr. Phil"), psychologist and TV-show host

Samuel was a mid-level manager at a prestigious New York City museum. He attended a day-long workshop I conducted on assertiveness, and during the program he barely spoke, though he did take copious notes. At the end of the day he hung back and waited for everyone else to leave, then approached me. He expressed his deep frustrations about feeling overwhelmed when navigating the dinners, conferences, and other business and social functions he was required to attend as a member of the museum's development team, a position to which he had recently been promoted.

As he told me about his goals for the museum, his passion for his work was clear, so I was shocked when he admitted that he was thinking about quitting. He said that he thought his networking ineptitude would hurt the museum, and that therefore he was the wrong person for the job. I voiced my hunch that this networking apprehension was something he could overcome. He seemed encouraged by my words. In order to devise a plan to try to help him deal with the challenges, I needed to see him in action to better understand his unease. So he invited me to attend an upcoming fund-raising event at the museum, where I could assess his handling of the situation myself. I accepted the offer.

No sooner had I arrived at the event when I was suddenly jarred by a loud bark of laughter. I turned to find out who made the noise, and was startled to see that it was Samuel. I couldn't believe that the harsh, off-putting sound I just heard had come from the same mild-mannered person I'd been speaking with just a few days earlier.

As the night continued, Samuel kept a brittle smile plastered on his face. Every now and then he caught my eye and raised his eyebrows to indicate he was "working the crowd." But by the end of the night, he looked exhausted by the strain of the immense effort he had put forth. And that was just the problem—he had been "working it," as in *working at it,* rather than just being, talking, listening, sharing.

When we spoke about the evening afterward, he was disheartened, if not surprised, to learn that I had seen through the smile. "But I was trying so hard to be engaging," he explained, "to act as it seems a successful person in my position would."

"I know," I responded. "That's the problem."

When we come from an authentic, genuine place in ourselves, our efforts to connect with people work to their fullest. Our relationships develop more easily and last longer, and we feel better about the people we've brought into our lives and our work.

I've spent time coaching students on how to prepare for one of the most fundamental business interactions, the job interview. I remember watching again and again as one of my students, Raj, froze while tackling the task. He had a dry sense of humor and could chat easily in casual conversation, but as soon as we'd start doing a mock interview, his personality would disappear. I tried distracting him away from being self-conscious, but the second he realized I was posing an interview question he became stiff and formal and very, very serious. Even his word choices changed.

What I tried to impress upon him, and what he finally understood, is that there is no right or wrong way to interact with people; there is no one correct way to "be." What feels right for one person may feel all wrong for another. What matters most is what feels right for *you*. As soon as Raj started being himself in our mock interviews, he was able to think more flexibly and respond more quickly and just generally become far more engaging. His likability was coming through.

Be You, Be Real, Be *Authentic*

What does it mean to be authentic? The particulars are different for each of us, of course, because we all have different attitudes, behaviors, beliefs, skill sets, knowledge, goals, and values. In a general sense, though, authenticity is the same for everyone: It is about being your true self. This is the *law of authenticity*: The real you is the best you.

Being your authentic self feels natural, so much so that when you experience it you probably don't even notice it. On the flip side, we all know it when we're not being our natural selves. We feel uncomfortable, awkward even, perhaps unconfident and stressed, and more often than not, after being in a situation where we don't feel as if we are being our true selves, we'll feel drained. There is a difference between tired and drained. Tired is a physical state. But that drained, emptied-out feeling comes from the mental effort of forcing yourself to act in a way that is not natural for you, when you are doing something that doesn't feel quite right, something that feels inauthentic.

What is it that goes through our minds when we are not being ourselves? Over the years I have asked many people this question and the most frequent answers are:

- I don't like this situation, but I'm trying to be polite about it.
- I don't like this person, but I'm trying to act in an appropriate way.
- I need to act more like a successful person does.
- If people don't respond positively to me, at least I'll have an excuse if I don't act like myself.
- I am uncomfortable and don't know what to do about it.

And what is consistent about all these responses? They either represent things we feel we *should* do or a general fear of feeling vulnerable. We put on a false face when, for whatever reasons, we dread a situation or feel we are not up to it.

Authenticity is not just the subject of this first chapter, it is the guiding principle of the book. As you read through the other chapters you will discover that authenticity is woven into all the other laws. It is the keystone to likability, because it gets at its essence: The real you is the best you, and it's the most powerful tool for forming real connections.

LIVE THE LAW: *WHEN AM I ME?*

To start identifying, in an explicit way, what it means to be your authentic self, pay attention to how you feel at the beginning of a new interaction and how you feel at the end of it.

- If you experience a sense of dread, stop and ask yourself: Exactly what is it that provokes the dread. Is it a person, the task at hand, the environment?

- If you experience ease, again ask yourself: What is it about the circumstances that allow me to feel relaxed?

Whatever your internal responses to a situation, analyze what they were and why you had them. Your answers should reveal information about the kinds of experiences that prompt you to shy away from representing your true self, and those in which you feel effortlessly authentic. Use these perceptions about what feels naturally right and true as your "home base" knowledge, returning to it when you need to reconnect with what authenticity means for you.

Why Authenticity Matters

Let's go back to Samuel for a minute. When he first spoke to me about the museum's fund-raising efforts and the expansion plans behind them, he conveyed his excitement in a genuine, forthright way. His sincerity truly moved me. But a few days later, when I saw him at an actual museum event, it was clear from his plastered-on smile and barking laugh that something about the situation made him deeply uncomfortable. As a result, his real passion for his job and his commitment to the museum were not being conveyed to the very people—the potential donors—he needed to reach.

Authenticity is who you are—your honest reactions, your natural energy. Sharing what is real about you is the key to building real relationships with others. When you show your authentic self, people will respond in kind, laying the bedrock for mutual understanding, connections, and growth.

How Do You Do It?

The beauty of the law of authenticity is in its simplicity: Don't try, just be. Of course, embracing this simple truth can be easier said than done. In our fast-paced lives, we tend to tear through situations without giving them much thought, and so we might not even be aware of when we are and aren't being authentic. Even when we realize we are not genuinely being ourselves—when we are faking an attitude that we think is "better" than the one we truly feel, or sleepwalking through a situation because we think we don't have time to slow down and be fully present—it can be difficult to stop these behaviors. But the secret is to just stop trying to be who you think you "should" be, whether that's the too-busy-for-the-small-stuff boss or the acquiescent new hire who doesn't feel quite comfortable giving opinions. Quit monitoring or premeditating your actions. *Don't think, just be.*

In my rare downtime, my guilty pleasure is watching reality TV shows. So many of them are such primal struggles between personality types, and I find it fascinating to see the dramas play out. When I think about why I root for certain contestants and not others, the answer is always the same: The characters I'm drawn to are being real. On one show, there was the contestant who spoke a mile a minute, a trait that could sometimes be annoying. She knew she had this trait and tried to manage it, but she inevitably wound up babbling rapidly and excitedly in the end. Even though some of the other contestants were irritated by her chattering, because this quality was a natural part of her, and because she accepted it and had a sense of humor about it, it was part of her authentic charm. On another show there was a pretty girl who at first seemed like she'd be the stuck-up ice queen, the obvious target of envy and attention who'd polarize the whole group. It turned out, though, that she was a total goofball. She let her goofiness come out naturally and was completely okay with it, and on top of it, she was not self-conscious about her good looks. This combination made her entirely likable.

After I debriefed Samuel about his inauthentic behavior at the museum event, I continued coaching him on how to identify his weaknesses and harness his strengths when faced with similar situations. During one of our most useful exercises, we reflected on how children often don't censor their behavior, and their authentic selves naturally shine through. I shared a story about a friend of mine who had been a principal at an elementary school and who sported a rather shockingly unnatural head of red hair. She could always tell what the children thought of her hairdos because they would just blurt it right out. "I like your new hair color, it matches my raincoat!" they'd say, or "Why did you do *that* to your hair?" Any time she told these stories she beamed in awe at the kids' raw honesty.

Granted, Samuel and I weren't aiming for such childlike honesty that he'd be howling in laughter at the sight of a museum patron's kooky hat, but we *were* trying to reconnect with that unfettered experience of being a child, before the adult in us started modifying itself based on what it thought the bigger world wanted. We were trying to think back on a time that preceded grown-up responsibilities and concerns, to a time when our emotions, intentions, and behaviors were largely unfiltered.

Once Samuel was able to reconnect with what naturally made him feel at ease, he realized that although he dreaded being in a large crowd and feeling the need to be the life of the party, he was completely comfortable talking one-on-one or in very small groups, and under these conditions he could easily engage patrons and potential patrons in meaningful discussions about the museum.

LIVE THE LAW: *THE AUTHENTICITY TEST*

When you're in a situation that is making you feel uncomfortable or disconnected, take a moment to ask yourself: Am I being me? If the answer is "Yes," terrific, forge on. Sometimes feeling disconnected just means that you need to refocus your attention to reconnect in a genuine way. And your discomfort with the situation may stem from pushing yourself in a positive way; under these circumstances, feeling uncomfortable is being authentic.

But if your answer to the question is "No," then your next question needs to be, Why?

- Are you actively changing your behavior because of how you think you should act?

- Is there something about the situation that makes you feel nervous or inadequate or unprepared?

Take a deep breath and reconnect with that part of you that feels authentic and honest. Ask yourself, "What's the worst that can happen?" You'll find that usually the answer isn't that bad. Remind yourself what you can contribute to the situation. Conveying your genuine self will ground you regardless of outcome.

Make the Friends You Want to Make

On day one of my first year of business school, my classmates and I were divided into groups of sixty-five people, called clusters. The members of a cluster share every single class for the first year, so naturally cliques form.

My cluster coalesced around a few subgroups that were delineated by commonalities such as geographic background, financial upbringing, or preferred career path. The two groups with which I found myself most involved revolved around a guy from Boston and one from Brooklyn. The Boston group was the polo-shirt-and-khaki-pants crowd. Their mannerisms and humor were more refined and formal, and they appeared to enjoy an elite way of life, with seemingly endless social and business connections. Then there was the Brooklyn crew epitomized by a Brooklyn boy named

Dean (aka Dino), decidedly not refined and proud of it. They hadn't had as many advantages growing up as the Boston gang had, and they were louder, rowdier, often bantering back and forth in a hilarious and off-color way.

There was a clear distinction between the two groups, but both were friendly toward me. I liked people in both circles and could have gravitated toward either. Perhaps if I'd been thinking strictly about which group could "do more for me" I would have made it an objective to become part of the elite, wealthy group. I probably would have gained access to extremely useful contacts (and I definitely would have been invited to some great vacations in the Hamptons), but something about the group's refined tone didn't quite jibe with my natural personality. When I hung out with the Boston crowd, I found myself feeling as if I had to censor my boisterous, extroverted nature. The relationships I had with that group felt a bit forced and tenuous at times. When I spent time with the Brooklyn group I found that I was simply more comfortable, happier, and relaxed. I still consider many from the Boston group friends. However, the Brooklyn relationships grew much stronger simply because I could just be myself.

When I started spending time with Brooklyn Dino's gang, I wasn't looking for anything beyond friendships and shared interests, yet the relationships I developed back then continue to enrich my life and my work. Years later, when I called Dino to tell him that I'd been laid off, I was reaching out as a friend. I didn't expect his response to be "Come work here"—which is exactly what I did, less than one week after that call. People from the Brooklyn group are more than friends; they have become important clients, colleagues, referrals, and sources of information for me, both professionally and personally. And I wasn't looking for any of these outcomes when I befriended them.

So here's the point: Cultivate the connections that you *want* to have, not the ones you think you *should* have. Build relationships with the people you enjoy, based on your authentic experiences of them—that is, when you are being your authentic *you*. The rest will follow. The network that you create is the one that will sustain you.

LIVE THE LAW: *DO IT, REFRAME IT, OR DELETE IT*

When you make the choices you want to make, not the ones you think you *should* make, you allow your authentic self to emerge. It's not just about choosing the situations you want to partake in, but also about deciding how to respond to events once they are in motion.

There are four basic attitudes that we bring to each situation, and they can reaffirm what is authentic for us or help us readjust our approaches to let the authentic in.

Get To: This is how you think about the things that make you feel genuinely giddy, alert, and excited.

Want To: These are the things that you freely choose to do, even though choosing and achieving them is not always easy.

Have To: These are the things you dread, even though they must be done.

Should: These are the things that society, your company, or some other outside force seems to think it would be good for you to do, and even though you may agree with those notions, the things in this category are not ones you *want* to do, but rather ones you feel obligated to do.

To put these attitudes to the test, choose anything from your to-do list or your upcoming calendar of events and then quickly, without thinking about it, jot down the attitude that most fits how you feel about the task: Get To, Want To, Have To, or Should. You'll be surprised by how much this simple exercise reveals. For instance, if you have an upcoming speaking engagement at a local high school, you could find yourself thinking, *I **get to** speak to 400 lively teenagers, or I **have to** speak to 400 rowdy teenagers.* Same situation, different attitudes. Once you know what your attitude is, you can consider your options and decide what to do about it.

OPTION 1: DO IT

If you have a Get To or Want To attitude toward a situation, then choosing to do it is easy. If your attitude is Have To or Should, you may still need to figure out how to get it done if the task is important enough, even if the authentic desire to do it isn't really there. Under these circumstances, seek a way to accomplish the task that will let you stay true to yourself. In Samuel's case, he has to not only attend fund-raisers, but also mingle with guests. This is a key part of his job, regardless of how uncomfortable it makes him. But instead of trying to be the life of the party and imposing an unnatural role on himself, he now opts to talk with smaller groups, an approach that makes him both more comfortable and much more effective. He has taken a Have To job assignment and found ways to do it while remaining authentic and real.

OPTION 2: REFRAME IT

Sometimes it's possible—and powerful—to take a Have To or Should situation and approach it from a new angle, literally changing the way you view it. For instance, if Samuel's original attitude toward a party was, "I have to attend the fund-raiser and mingle with guests," he could reframe it by saying, "I want to tell people about all the amazing things the museum has planned." By reframing a difficult or dreaded situation, you can focus on the aspects of it that make you feel good and energized, recasting it as a Get To or Want To.

OPTION 3: DELETE IT

It's not always possible to just hit "delete" on something you don't want to do. There are things that simply must get done, and in those cases you need to do them with as much presence as possible. But before you resign yourself to suffering through absolutely every Have To or Should situation, take a good second look at them. Often we have so deeply bought into the Have To or Should mentality that it dominates our thinking and clouds our true selves to the point where we end up bowing to the pressure. But, if you see that a Have To or Should task isn't actually necessary, and that completing it would mean just going through the motions, then delete it from your list. If you can't greet the task with authentic and positive energy, you are not making the best use of your time or yourself.

Good News for the Introverts

Introverts usually think that making connections and building relationships is something that comes more naturally for extroverts. The average extrovert probably wouldn't agree or disagree with this belief; the extrovert simply wouldn't think about it, because extroverts are often too busy being themselves to stop and analyze what they are doing. Contrary to what introverts might think, extroverts face their own challenges connecting (this topic is examined in greater detail in Chapter 3).

But for now, introverts should know that they can feel completely at ease in business and social situations too, and that being introverted can be a strength. Introverts are often naturally equipped to initiate connections because they tend to be good listeners. If you are an introvert, the key is to listen to your own rhythms. Don't try to emulate your wildly gregarious colleagues; instead, pay attention to what makes *you* comfortable. Do you get tired after a long night of chitchat? It's okay to leave a function on the early side, to connect with whomever you need to and then bow out before the shindig dies down. When you are part of a group conversation, do you prefer to listen to others and only speak up when you have something to say? Then by all means, do just that, it's entirely fine. In terms of behaviors, whatever *you* decide feels authentic and true is what is okay.

My friend Julie is an introvert and normally quite shy. When a guy she'd been dating, and really liked, invited her to dinner to meet his parents, she told me that she smilingly accepted, but inside she felt totally nauseous. "How am I going to get through this dinner?" she asked me. "What should I do?" When I answered, "What about just being yourself?" she looked at me as if I had ten heads. Clearly that wasn't something she felt would come naturally to her in the situation. She was worried that she might not live up to his parents' expectations, and she didn't know how to come across as the perfect girlfriend. "If you feel like being quiet and waiting for someone else to start the conversation, wait. You're allowed," I said. A light went on in her eyes, as if suddenly understanding that she could give herself permission to just be herself.

The next time I checked in with her, I asked how the dinner had gone. "It was actually fine," she said calmly. "We may not have become super close on the first meeting, but I didn't feel like an idiot for being shy. To be honest, it was a revelation for me. I realized that being shy is no big deal. I don't have to struggle to cover it up; I can accept myself for it and be okay in new situations, even if they're still a bit uncomfortable."

When You Need to Fake It, Make It Real

Sometimes we find ourselves in situations with people we simply don't like, for whatever reasons. In nonprofessional settings these situations can be straightforward to deal with, because often all you have to do is just minimize contact with that person. In business settings, though, these situations can be more of a challenge. When faced with a difficult colleague, how do you change a contentious dynamic into a productive one?

For me, these challenges are often thorniest in the realm of performance appraisals. Almost as soon as I started managing direct reports in my career, I realized there would be times when I'd have to review troublesome colleagues who angered me because they were underperforming, or frustrated me because their poor social skills made it tough for everyone else to work with them. But how could I evaluate their performance in a way that would enhance the professional environment, not damage it?

My first full-time job was at an accounting firm. During my second year I was managing an auditing team that included a young guy named Kevin. And Kevin just didn't get it. The demands of the project were intense and the time frame was tight, so it was important that everyone perform optimally. Still, at the end of each round of work there would be numerous tasks that Kevin had messed up, and the rest of us had to put in a good amount of extra time cleaning up after him. Needless to say, this made me extremely frustrated.

At the end of the audit I had to give Kevin a performance review. I was angry about the extra work he caused for me and others, but I couldn't go into the performance review feeling bitter about him, because that would have demonstrated poor management skills and not contributed anything positive to the situation.

So what did I do? After much grappling and some sleepless nights, I finally found the good. I thought extensively about the conundrum of Kevin and realized that although he did have some deficits, if I was going to be honest, he also had some incredible strengths. He came to the office every day with a smile on his face, and he had established the best rapport of any of us with the client. If pieces of information needed to be procured, Kevin was always the first one to be able to get them. So I went into Kevin's review with both the pluses and minuses of his performance in mind, and we were able to discuss them honestly.

Through this open dialogue we realized that there were things about his current situation that didn't feel right for him, either, so we devised a work plan that would keep him in the company but get him trained in a department that was a better fit for him. We instituted the plan, and his professional life thrived. That was a powerful lesson for me. It taught me that an important part of being authentic is staying open to finding what makes others authentic as well. Despite my initial resistance and doubts, I found a way to connect with Kevin's authentic assets and strengths, and this benefited us both.

LIVE THE LAW: *FIND THE GOOD*

Sometimes we are in situations where we have to deal with people we may not like. Our gut reaction may be to try hiding our true feelings, while in our minds we fume about how irritating the person in question is. The problem, of course, is that these attempts to hide our true feelings require us to be fake, and more often than not, such behaviors are completely transparent. For goodness sake, when dealing with a difficult acquaintance or colleague, don't plaster on a forced smile or get all sugary sweet trying to hide your venom, and don't try to ignore someone who gets under your skin.

Instead, find the good! Often, people who have qualities opposite from ours make us uncomfortable and, conversely, people who are too similar to us can make us flinch. Both these situations create great opportunities for appreciating ourselves and those around us.

- Can you find compassion and understanding for the person whose strengths might be your own weaknesses?

- Can you find compassion and understanding for the person who reflects things back to you about yourself that you'd rather not face?

- Just as important, in either situation, can you find compassion and understanding for yourself?

With unbiased eyes, look at the person who's under your skin and find something that you can admire or appreciate. Identifying these traits will transform your experience of that person, and your conversational ease and more relaxed body language will come from an authentic place. You don't need to become best friends with the person, but you don't need to keep acting in ways that might create or exacerbate a bad situation, either. When you can focus on what you truly do appreciate about other people, their likability—and yours—will naturally increase.

The Networking Application

"Being authentic" is not a permission slip to be rude, obnoxious, or inappropriate. It means connecting with your true self and letting it shine through so that others can connect with you, too. It means listening to your inner dialogue and internally noting your initial, unfiltered responses to things. It also means taking situations that seem daunting, uncomfortable, or just plain difficult and finding ways to approach them with the true, engaged you. Is there a networking event you are dreading, but feel you should attend? If it's something you should but don't have to do, delete it and let yourself off the hook. If it is in fact imperative that you attend the event, reframe it so that you are attending it *your* way, converting it into something you want to do or are happy to get to do. Think about Samuel: He reframed his predicament of dreading his employer's fund-raising events by focusing on smaller groups at those events, not only setting up situations for himself that felt more natural but also creating opportunities for real communication.

Being authentic will get you where you need and want to go, and it will be your path to building the most meaningful and enriching connections with others.

Refresh Your Memory

The Law of Authenticity. The real you is the best you.

Be Your True Self. The "right" way to be is what feels right for *you*, whether that's leaving an event early or staying all night, being the life of the party or mingling in smaller groups. Do what feels authentic for you, and people will respond positively.

Make the Connections *You* Want to Make. The relationships you genuinely care about are the ones that will form the strongest network you can build.

Do It, Reframe It, or Delete It. Understand your choices and adjust your attitudes to reflect your authentic self. When there are things you Have To or Should do, convert them into things you Get To or Want To do; in other words, look for something in the situation that feels real and more acceptable to you. If there are any Have Tos or Shoulds that aren't imperative, delete them. You have choices!

When You Need to Fake It, Make It Real. Finding the good in difficult situations or personalities allows for more productive and positive interactions.

2

The Law of Self-Image

"An individual's self-concept is the core of his personality. It affects every aspect of human behavior: the ability to learn, the capacity to grow and change. A strong, positive self-image is the best possible preparation for success in life."

—Dr. Joyce Brothers, psychologist

There is one particular client, Sandy, who stands out for me from my days as a career coach. Even though the details of her story were, of course, unique to her, the fears she had about her professional life were representative of the basic fears and struggles of many of my clients, especially those faced with reinventing themselves mid-career due to a poor economy or those returning to the workforce after many years away.

Sandy was a smart, attractive, college-educated woman who was in her early fifties when we started working together. She had spent most of the previous twenty years living in a small Midwestern town, raising four children while her husband held down the same job he'd had since before the kids were born. When her husband got laid off, Sandy found herself needing to return to the workplace for the first time in nearly two decades.

She timidly entered my office and waited for permission before taking a seat. As I reached for her résumé, the look on her face was a mixture of fear and desperation, with just the slightest glimmer of hope. I could almost hear her thoughts: *I am a lost cause, but maybe you can fix me.*

After only a few moments of conversation, she blurted out, "I have a college degree, but it's been years since my last job outside the home, and now I'm over fifty." The statement was somewhere between a confession and an apology. She explained that before her children were born, she'd worked as a services coordinator for a major nonprofit, but nowadays she felt as if she had no skills to offer in a workplace environment. As our conversation continued, her body language and tone of voice, even more than her words, revealed how she felt about herself. She sat compactly in the chair as if she were afraid to take up too much space, and she had trouble maintaining eye contact with me. Her voice was hushed and sounded resigned. But what I heard Sandy screaming loud and clear was, "I'm not worthy. I'm not good enough. Everyone else is more qualified than me."

Realizing how her poor self-image must be affecting her job search, I said, "Let's forget about what you haven't done and talk about what you have done." She shifted in her seat and sat up a little straighter, then began recounting some of the ways she'd been involved in her children's schools. She talked about her work with the PTA, and how she had served as the parent liaison for several of her children's classes. Her pride in these tasks was clear, and she actually beamed when she explained how she had never missed a game or a dance recital. She grew animated when she described how expertly she coordinated the family's schedules, ensuring that everyone was always on time. At the end of each anecdote, though, she would shrug off my enthusiasm, minimizing her contributions with such responses as, "It was not really a big deal," or "Well, that's just what moms do."

The going was at times arduous because Sandy's lack of belief in her professional worth was deeply entrenched, but she was committed to the process. Slowly but surely, we outlined how the skills she'd developed in the past few decades could be applied to the workplace, and she began to see and, even more important, believe in her value.

As a professor at a leading business school, I strive to instill in my students a few key tenets. Chief among them is that "perception is reality." I know that this maxim may sound cliché, but it is also unequivocally true. If the ways you perceive other people become your reality about them, then how you perceive yourself is your reality about you. What you believe about your strengths, weaknesses, knowledge, and skills is what you transmit to the outside world.

A few years ago I had a part-time MBA student named Dave who was a tax controller in his day job. Whenever we did class presentations, Dave was unfailingly enthusiastic about and supportive of his fellow students, pointing out the positive aspects of a presentation even when it had been less than stellar. But when it came to his own performance, Dave had nothing but harsh self-criticism. The rest of his coursework was strong, but he stumbled when it came to giving his presentation to the group. He simply believed that he couldn't do it well.

The good news is that because our perceptions of ourselves create our realities, we have the power to change these perceptions in wholly positive ways. For Dave, it took viewing several videos of himself making a presentation to realize that he didn't look as nervous as he felt. I have since received an exuberant e-mail from Dave, telling me that at the last minute he had to fill in for a senior colleague and deliver a presentation to an important client. He was extremely nervous going into the meeting, but he worked hard to prepare and was able to deliver the presentation in a confident manner that impressed the client as well as his boss. "I kept remembering how nervous I was in your class while presenting, but that I looked and sounded all right on camera. And that's what got me through it," he wrote to me, adding, "And I even remembered to smile." Dave had changed his perception of his own reality, and his positive self-image was the conduit for strong connection and communication in a crucial situation.

You Have to Like You First!

To make meaningful connections in an authentic way, you have to project the best parts of your true self. In other words, before you expect others to like you, *you* have to like you—that is the *law of self-image*. Many of us are aware of our basic strengths, and can often exude confidence in a variety of situations, but even the most self-assured among us have our moments of self-doubt. The trick is learning how to work through them. One top executive I know confided to me that it took him years to feel as if he was really worthy of playing with "the big dogs." He recounted how, as he rose up the corporate ladder, he would often find himself sitting in a meeting, looking around and thinking, "Wow, my colleagues are really on top of their game. Can I hold my own with them?" Each time, he took these moments of self-doubt as a challenge to reassess his value and worth and strengthen his self-image by reconnecting with what he knew he *could* contribute to his workplace, not what he couldn't. Over time he trained himself to embody this awareness of his assets. His career thrived apace with his positive self-image.

Most of us are much harder on ourselves than we are on other people. We would agree that it is not right to be mean or petty or judgmental toward other people—so why is it okay when we do that to ourselves? Perception is reality, and self-image is self-perception. When we don't follow up with potential clients because we assume that they have better offers or won't switch to another business provider, when we don't pursue a new position because we assume that there are stronger candidates, we are affirming our negative assumptions as our reality. When you find yourself having self-doubting or self-sabotaging thoughts, you need to ask yourself, "Do I want to be right about this? Right about not landing the client or not getting the job?" If your answer is "No," then you need to change your reality.

Why Self-Image Matters

Before Sandy and I began our coaching sessions, she'd applied to a few jobs but hadn't landed any first interviews. I was dismayed to learn this, but I wasn't surprised. It is all but impossible to make someone else believe in your qualifications and value if you don't first believe in them yourself.

Negative self-perceptions can adversely impact our productivity, our decisions, and even, when taken to extremes, our health. So why do we hold onto negative self-perceptions? There is often something to be gained from indulging in these thought patterns. It may be an instinct to protect ourselves against failure or to avoid repeating past mistakes, a desire not to threaten those around us by upsetting the status quo. Holding ourselves back may keep us safe, but it also means sacrificing how much we can grow and limiting what we can achieve. Creating a positive self-image doesn't mean eradicating all doubts and attaining perfection. Confidence comes from managing our self-doubts and accepting the fact that we are working on bettering our imperfections, even while appreciating these imperfections as qualities that make us unique and likable.

Once when I was riding the subway, there was a very full-figured twenty-something woman in the same car as me, and when I glanced over at her I was startled by her outrageous outfit. She looked like a 1970s disco queen, with a low-cut turquoise top, gold spiked heels, and big brash jewelry. My first thought was, "What is she *thinking?*" But then I looked at her face, and suddenly the outfit seemed entirely fetching. She stood there holding the rail, confident and calm, a sparkle in her eye indicating that she knew she looked good, and she did. She was completely comfortable in her own skin, extra tummy rolls and all, and she was showing the world that she thought she was one hot mamma. And as a result she *was* one hot momma. What we think about ourselves is who we are.

See the You That You Already Are

In the thick of our career coaching sessions, I stopped Sandy at one point and asked her flat out, "So what *are* you good at?" She stared at me blankly. When she didn't fill the silence, the conversation continued like this:

Me: I bet that you are very responsible.

Sandy (hesitating): Well, sure, if you ask me to do something, I get it done. I meet my deadlines.

Me: Okay, great, you are responsible. You believe that, right? (**She nodded.**) Now let's find another word. Tell me something else that you're good at.

Sandy (thinking for a moment, then begrudgingly): Well, I am organized. I always know where everything is, and friends frequently ask me to help them devise their own organizing systems. (**She watched as I added "organized" to our growing list.**)

I'm really good at that stuff. You should see my filing cabinet!

Me (looking at the job description and hunting for another word): Would you describe yourself as strategic?

Sandy (balking and rolling her eyes): No way!

Me: Well, hold on, how do you define "strategic"?

Sandy (shrugging): I don't know, I guess I picture some CEO sitting behind a desk making big corporate decisions.

Me: So would you define "strategic" as someone who makes important decisions that impact the well-being of others? Isn't that what you do for your family every day?

At this point Sandy was slowly beginning to comprehend where I was going. She then told me about how she'd helped her daughter choose a college and evaluate the myriad factors that go into such a life-defining decision, and how she assisted her daughter with the scholarship applications that eventually enabled her to attend her first-choice school. At the end of this account she laughed as the import of it all dawned on her. We added "strategic" to our words list.

Most people aren't this determined to bring themselves down. Sandy's negative self-image was on the extreme side, to be sure, but because of that she quite dramatically displayed what happens when negative self-perceptions start turning into positive ones. As our conversation continued, Sandy came up with more and more words that she felt truly described her, and as she did so her entire presence was transformed. She no longer sat slouched with rounded shoulders, physically minimizing herself. She grew animated as she singled out words that she could embrace as descriptions of herself. In short, she was choosing her words.

LIVE THE LAW: CHOOSE YOUR WORDS

This activity is about identifying the best words that define you. The resulting description of your strengths will be one that is not only true, but one you can truly believe. Here are the steps:

1. **Free Write.** Grab a pen and a piece of paper and for five minutes write down all the positive adjectives you can think of that describe you, then think about how you display or embody those qualities. Don't censor yourself and don't stop writing, just keep the pen moving the whole time. If you get stuck, rewrite the words you've already jotted down. Cast the net wide. Don't just focus on your work qualities, but on all aspects of your life. Do the kids on the soccer team that you coach always come to you when they've messed up on the field because they know you'll have a supportive, encouraging word? Do your friends enlist your help with home fix-it repairs because they know you'll not only do it, but you'll explain to them how to do it without making them feel stupid? Write it all down. When the time is up, put down the pen and read what you wrote. Then read it again.

2. **Feedback.** We are often blind to our own best qualities, even when they are obvious to others around us. Gather information by asking people to describe you. Choose people who know you well in addition to more casual acquaintances. Try out these different questions or come up with your own:

   - How would you describe me?

   - What do you consider my best qualities and strengths?

   - If you could choose just one positive word to define me, what would it be?

   If you are hesitant to ask such open-ended questions, you might offer an attribute for the person to agree or disagree with. And if you are unclear about or surprised by any of the responses, ask for clarification. Why did a person choose that word to describe you? Can the person give an example of a time when you embodied that word or displayed that quality? Make sure you understand the basis of the feedback. Get convinced.

When given this assignment, one of my clients decided to also query people with whom he didn't get along. His reasoning? "If they could name something positive about me, then I must really possess that quality." If one of these people gave him feedback that didn't resonate with him at all, he considered the source, shrugged it off, and moved on. An interesting strategy to consider.

3. **Choose.** Look at what you wrote about yourself against the feedback you've gathered from others, and choose the words that resonate most strongly with you. You have just chosen your words. And they are all true.

Talk to Yourself, but Be Nice!

We all talk to ourselves, and when we keep telling ourselves something we eventually begin to believe it. This is such a fundamental truth that psychologists have come up with a clinical term for it: self-talk. The concept has proved particularly useful in the field of sports psychology, and numerous studies have shown time and again that the differences between negative self-talk and positive self-talk have everything to do with how athletes perform. Negative self-talk can naturally arise when encountering obstacles, as we all know, and professional athletes are no exception to this rule. But learning how to transform these harsh thoughts into self-encouragement and positive self-talk is what makes the best athletes succeed.

In one sports medicine study, Daniel Gould, Kenneth Hodge, Kirsten Peterson, and John Giannini demonstrated how winning coaches prepared their athletes for competition by modeling self-confidence and teaching athletes to convert detrimental self-criticism into empowering self-belief.[1] In another important study, Dr. Joan A. Finn showed how positive self-talk reduces anxiety, boosts confidence, and increases performance.[2]

Thoughts such as "I'm no good at that," "I have nothing to offer," "It's too hard, I can't do it," and "If I try it, I'll look ridiculous" become true when you play them over and over in your head in a nonstop loop. Others pick up on and believe what you project and believe about yourself. To increase your authentic likability and forge successful connections, harnessing positive self-talk is key. And the only one who can do that is you.

LIVE THE LAW: *HOW NICE ARE YOU TO YOU?*

What is your inner voice saying to you? To find out, track it for a week, marking down every self-thought you can. How many times did you give yourself credit for something and mentally pat yourself on the back? For each instance, give yourself a point. How many times did you discourage or gang up on yourself? For each of those cases, subtract a point. If a thought started off as negative but you were able to convert it into something positive, give yourself two points.

At the end of the week, tally your points. Did you end the week in the positive column? Can you increase your score next week? Determine whether or not you are happy with the results. If not, get proactive about changing your perceptions and embracing your good. Be *nice*. Here are some ideas that can help you:

- **Keep a Success File.** Every time someone says something nice about you, compliments your work, or sends an e-mail of appreciation, write it down or print it out and put it in a folder. You may even send yourself a quick e-mail when you remember something of which you're particularly proud. It is all too easy to forget your positive accomplishments when you're worried instead about what's wrong. Pull out the file on a regular basis and leaf through your successes to remind yourself of the good you achieve.

- **Revisit Your Accomplishments.** A friend of mine who is extremely successful and appears outwardly confident is, in fact, impacted easily by small criticisms and mistakes. When she feels as if she's getting too down on herself, she closes her office door, pulls out her journal, and writes down everything she knows she is good at, resetting her self-talk to the positive thoughts that eventually get her where she wants and needs to be.

Change Your Tune

I have always wanted to write a book. For years I composed outlines and came up with catchy titles, but the projects never went any further than that. In my head I had all sorts of reasons why my book-writing dream couldn't come true: "You don't have enough to say," "It's just too hard," "You don't know how," "No one will buy it."

I have always been self-confident, yet that didn't stop these thoughts from permeating my mind. The results of my negative self-talk? For years I took no action at all. To get to the place where I could tackle the task—to the place where you could be sitting there, reading this text—I had to change my self-talk. It was a process of continually reminding myself that what I said to myself was entirely up to me. Along the way I learned that changing my self-talk from negative to positive was not a Pollyannaish, look-in-the-mirror-and-do-your-daily-affirmations endeavor. It was a series of actionable steps that helped me reprogram my perceptions and my sense of self-ability so that I had the courage to sit down at my desk each day and face the scary blank page, regardless of the fears welling up inside me. Of course, self-doubts continued to creep in, and they still do; that is only natural, but I was able to take steps to manage my negative self-talk and the influence it had over me, which freed me to accomplish something difficult that I'd long set out to do.

Similarly, Dave, my former student, had been doggedly struggling for a long while to improve his presentations performance. Once he learned to listen to the inner voices that were telling him he *could* speak effectively in front of a crowd, and stopped paying as much attention to the voices telling him he *couldn't* do it, he was able to wow the client, impress his boss, and, most important, recognize his own professional growth. He wrote to me, "While I was presenting I was able to hold an image in my head of myself as calm and confident, and that made all the difference."

Now that you've gone through the exercise (Live the Law: How Nice Are You to You?) and you have a handle on the content of your negative self-messages, you can start developing the positive messages that will replace them. I've learned that three techniques are particularly useful in this process:

1. Be your own best friend.
2. Frame a positive picture.
3. Celebrate the small stuff.

Be Your Own Best Friend

Think back to a time when you've had a cycle of negative self-thoughts running through your head, and then imagine your best friend feeling that way about himself and expressing those thoughts to you. What would you do? You would immediately start listing all your friend's wonderful qualities so that your friend's negative self-talk could be converted from mean and detrimental to helpful and productive.

Do this for yourself, too; be your own best friend. We all have that bully who appears on our shoulders, whispering nasty self-thoughts into our ears. On the opposite shoulder sits the cheerleader, the one who believes in our worth and reminds us of our successes, strengths, and goals. The next time the bully starts in on a rant, stop it in its tracks, think about what you want to hear instead, and kick the cheerleader into gear. Sandy's bully was yammering, "You are unqualified, inexperienced, and you will never get a job." With effort she learned to counter the bully with the cheerleader who reminded her, "You have so many skills you've gained from life experience. You are responsible, organized, and strategic in your decisions. An employer would be lucky to have you."

Over time the process gets easier. As you grow more aware of the negative self-thoughts rising up, you'll catch them earlier, pinpoint their alternatives, and become better at changing them into positive self-perceptions with powerful results.

Frame a Positive Picture

An important corollary to countering the negative self-talk is learning how to reframe it from bad to good. The glass is either half empty or half full, and remember that whatever your perspective, it is entirely your choice.

When you frame your actions around what you fear and what you think you can't do, those are the results you'll achieve. Reframing thoughts shifts your perspective from expected doom to intended success, impacting the outcomes of your decisions and actions. Embrace your possibilities, not your potential failures. You get what you expect.

The process of reframing has two aspects: internal and external.

Internal framing is similar to visualization in that you picture what you want and then mentally rehearse or practice how it might unfold. You coach yourself to think positively about your skill set, your strengths, a task you need to do. Positive thinking leads to positive outcomes.

With *external framing,* you take your internally framed thoughts and put words to them, sharing them with others to give them validity and weight.

At one point I had a colleague named Yael who was intent on making partner at our firm, even though she'd been there for only eight years and the normal partner track was thirteen years. Instead of giving in to an internal chorus of "Don't be ridiculous, you'll never make partner this soon; don't waste your time," Yael put her firm belief in her abilities in the front of her mind and flat out went for it. She wasn't obnoxious or overbearing about pursuing her goal; she was consistent, determined, and assured. She didn't make partner that first year, but she did in the second, becoming the only person in more than a decade to make partner in ten years. She had internally framed her self-thoughts and actions, and then externally framed them, keeping at it until the two were perfectly aligned.

LIVE THE LAW: *ACCENTUATE THE POSITIVE*

The words we choose to describe something—whether we say them out loud or in our own heads—impact how we view it. Words are the frames we put around the pictures in our minds, and framing plays a powerful role in creating self-perceptions. Choosing how we *re*frame our thoughts likewise impacts our actions and results. Shift your focus onto the good stuff, and the negative stuff falls away. To increase positive framing, try the following strategies:

- **Choose the positive take on something, not the negative.** It is easy to say what you are not going to do, but in the end that is just doing nothing. Instead, state what you are going to do, creating a clear vision of the actions you intend to take. As examples:

  I am working too slowly. I'll never finish this project. I should just give up.
  vs.
  I'm taking my time to make sure things are done correctly; I've worked really hard and I need to take a break.

- **Select strong, actionable verbs.** The verb you choose sets the tone for the action to follow. Action verbs create clarity about your goals and intended results:

  I am considering *what job I* may *apply for.*
  vs.
  I am deciding *what job I* will *apply for.*

- **Focus on what you can do, not on what you can't.** Fear of the unknown can be overwhelming and sometimes leaves us thinking, "I can't." But uttering those two words, "I can't," is a way of giving yourself permission to give up. By stating instead what you can do, you open up opportunities for creating results.

  I have never done this before and have no idea what to do. This is not going to go well.
  vs.
  I am excited that I get to work on something new. I may never have done this before, but I have several resources to leverage to ensure that it goes well.

- **Convert obstacles, challenges, and perceived failures into knowledge.** Kicking yourself when something goes wrong may seem like a justified response, but it accomplishes nothing. Instead, identify what you can learn from the mistake and commit to handling things differently the next time.

  It took me ten grueling years to finally get the courage to write a book.

  vs.

  This book was written at the right time, after I had acquired the experiences necessary to make it robust.

Start listening to yourself. Catching yourself in the act is the most powerful and influential time to reframe your thoughts. Just ask yourself, "How else can I view this situation, this person, or this action?"

Celebrate the Small Stuff

As I've already mentioned, one of my big dreams has long been to write this book. When I first conceived of it ten years ago, I could see the finish line, but the vastness of the work it would require to get there caused a huge dose of inertia to settle in. The project seemed so much bigger than me, and I felt incapable, overwhelmed, and not up to the task. Before I'd even begun I wanted to quit.

But then I started breaking down the process into individual steps, and suddenly I was able to embark on the journey. Step One: Settle on the book idea. Step Two: Research the publishing process. Step Three: Learn the components of a proposal, put out an ad for a proposal editor, and hire one. Step Four: Write the chapters; and so on. I rewarded myself each time I completed a step, to mark my enormous relief and sense of accomplishment. The rewards weren't always big ones—some were as simple as an hour of guilt-free TV watching or a phone call to a friend—but they helped me feel good about accomplishing my goals and excited to achieve the next ones. Somewhere along the way, my mindset changed from "Ack! I can't do this!" to "Yes, it's going to be difficult, but I know that I'm capable of it and it will get done!"

Progress feels good and has a profound effect on our thought patterns, and therefore on our productivity and our sense of self. Celebrate it!

Fake It Till You Make It Real

At first glance, "Fake it till you make it" seems to counsel inauthenticity, but that's not the true point of the saying, which is why I like to clear up the confusion by using, "Fake it till you make it *real.*" The purpose is to try on what it might look and feel like to perceive of ourselves in new ways, or to act differently than we're accustomed to. By stretching out of our comfort zones—or as some would say, "faking it"—we can grow comfortable with these new modes of thought and action until they eventually become normal or "real" to us.

When I went on my first client call with JPMorgan Chase, early in my career, I was still completely green. I didn't yet have a website or a company name (not to mention a business card), and I wondered how I was going to possibly convince this huge organization that I was knowledgeable and effective enough to hire. I had no track record to speak of, no real references, and I thought to myself, "Who am I kidding?"

But then I took that thought process one step further. "Okay," went my self-talk, "so how would I speak and carry myself if I had already been doing this job for years?" I tapped into the confidence that I knew was in there, stemming from my genuine excitement about the prospect of working for this client and all the ideas I'd already generated about how I might help the client, and I put that image firmly in my mind. Then I followed it, acting "as if" I was already where I was striving to be. I never would and did not lie during our initial meeting, but I did choose my words carefully, highlighting my confidence in my ability and underscoring the successful experiences (few as they were) that I already had. And I landed the client.

This is the same tactic Dave used to ace his client presentation, and it's the same way Yael made partner in an unprecedented short time. "Fake it till you make it real" is another way of actively reframing your thoughts, and by extension your actions, decisions, and motivations. Strengthening self-image is a process, and imagining the end goal is part of what helps get you there.

Working from the Outside In

Clothes may or may not make the man, but they are a powerful communicator of your inner state. If you wake up feeling tired and glum and dress in baggy, shapeless clothes to maximize comfort, you transmit that glumness to the world. On mornings when you feel energized and pull on something bright and colorful, you'll notice that that energy tends to stay with you throughout the day, and that people communicate a similar energy back to you. It's a challenge to feel alert and prepared when dressed for the couch. When you dress to feel put-together and sharp, other people will perceive you in this way, reflecting it back to you and strengthening the thoughts you have about yourself.

Self-image is the basis for how you experience—and are experienced by—the outside world. It is directly linked to the law of perception, which is explored in Chapter 3.

Refresh Your Memory

The Law of Self-Image. Before you can expect others to like you, *you* have to like you.

Perception Is Reality. Just as the ways you perceive other people become your reality about them, the ways you perceive yourself become your reality about you.

Be Nice to Yourself. This isn't just a warm-fuzzy idea, it's a scientific principle. Positive self-talk paves the way for authentic productivity and success.

Change Your Tune. Convert negative self-talk to a positive by reminding yourself regularly of your genuine accomplishments, reframing obstacles or challenges by creating clarity about your intended outcomes, and celebrating each step of the way.

Fake It Till You Make It Real. Acting "as if" you have already changed your thinking or achieved a desired goal is a powerful way to grow accustomed to new thought patterns and strategies. Keep acting "as if" until you have fully absorbed the new approach and made it real.

3

The Law of Perception

"One has not only an ability to perceive the world but an ability to alter one's perception of it; more simply, one can change things by the manner in which one looks at them."

—Tom Robbins, *Even Cowgirls Get the Blues*

There was a woman named Erica in my cluster at business school. While she did spend some time with my circle of friends, more often than not she stuck to herself, which I took as her being aloof. Erica was five feet eleven inches tall and gorgeous; in fact, she'd done a stint as a model. She was extremely smart and had held a prestigious financial job before business school, and on top of all that she was rich—not just a little rich, but extremely wealthy. The way she held herself apart from everyone seemed to indicate that she thought she was better than the rest of us.

Although I tried a few times to engage her in chitchat, she always seemed to blow me off, so after a while I just left her alone. Except for the smart part, she was the exact opposite of me. I was four feet ten, gregarious and social, and didn't grow up with buckets of money. "Maybe," I figured, "I'm just too different from her for her to have any interest in talking to me."

For spring break that first year I organized a trip to Jamaica. I would only be able to afford the trip myself if I sold all fourteen slots for it, so I promoted it heavily within my cluster, hoping all my friends would be able to go. And who do you think brought me the first check to hold a spot? Yup—Erica! "Ugh!" I thought, "I have to spend my hard-earned vacation with someone who treats me like I am invisible. Not my idea of fun." To make matters worse, the final tally was ten guys and four girls, so because of the way the accommodations were arranged all of us girls would be sharing a room together.

"Terrific," I thought, "So now I'm really stuck sharing my vacation with this snobby rich girl I have nothing in common with and who looks down her nose at me." Or at least that was my perception of the situation going into it.

During my years of coaching, I frequently heard clients express sentiments such as, "I don't see myself that way," and "I can't understand what I did to give them that impression." Usually it was because my clients were meeting with some workplace resistance when trying to advance their careers. What is it that creates a disconnect between how we perceive ourselves and how others perceive us? Understanding how our own perceptions are formed can give us some insight into how others form their perceptions of us. Once you get a handle on how perceptions are created and sustained, you can be more proactive about making the impressions you want to make and projecting your value outward so that other people recognize it. When you project your authentic self, people will respond to and connect with it. Perception is a core component of likability.

What's Your Impression?

I may not have told you this yet, but I am always right. And so are you, from your perspective. We've already seen in Chapter 2 that our perceptions of ourselves are our realities about ourselves, and of course the external corollary of this is true, too: Our perceptions of others are our realities about them. This is the *law of perception.* Whatever impressions a person gathers of you, as he consciously or unconsciously interprets your words and actions, become his reality about you. What we perceive is what we believe to be true.

Although we can't completely control other people's perceptions of us—after all, we bring our own unique mix of beliefs, personality, life experiences, and biases to bear when we form opinions about people—we can definitely impact these perceptions in positive rather than negative ways. One of the most important things to remember is that perceptions typically form quickly, within the first few minutes of meeting someone. It often takes only moments to have an instinctual reaction to someone and draw conclusions about that person. It is not that we form quick judgments intentionally, it is simply a natural way that people process new situations and encounters.

It is possible for these perceptions to change over time, of course, as two people come to know each other more fully, but first impressions are powerful. This is why the law of perception has a sublaw, the *law of first impressions*: It is far easier to make a good first impression than to change a bad one. As human beings, we love to be right. If my first impressions of you are that your energy level is tepid, more often than not I'll experience you that way on future occasions, fitting subsequent impressions of you into this tepid perception. I am proving myself right. It may take a while for me to change my perception of you enough to see that the real you is actually quite dynamic. So why not start off letting the real you come through? First impressions are critical.

Choose Your Perceptions

As it turned out, that spring break trip back then wasn't at all bad. In fact, it was phenomenal, in large part because Erica turned out to be great. During our first day in Jamaica, we were both lounging on rafts in the pool when the heavens opened up and it began to pour. We both started laughing at how sudden and dramatic the tropical storm was, and then we looked at one another, floating around in the rain, and laughed even harder. The setting was so completely different from the normal business school grind we'd been accustomed to that we were able to relax and let down our guard. We wound up having a fantastic time bumming around together during the trip, learning all about our very different upbringings, past relationships, and more, and by the time we got back to school, we were bona fide buddies.

I came to realize that my first impressions of Erica had been wrong, and I'd allowed these first impressions to harden into perception. Erica wasn't actually snotty and aloof; to my unbelievable surprise, she was shy. Once she came out of her shell, she was compassionate and warm, and she even had a rebellious streak. My perception of her had been totally off base.

There can be many reasons why our perceptions of people differ from who they really are, why authenticity and likability get "lost in translation," as it were. Let's look at three of them:

- Different Styles
- Inconsistent Communications
- Self-Doubt

Different Styles

We all have predispositions that come naturally to us. It can be as simple as which eye you close when you wink—there is no "correct" eye to use, it just comes down to what feels instinctively normal. Likewise we all have natural, innate tendencies when it comes to how we move through the world, how we communicate and interact with others, how we solve problems and make decisions. We all have different styles.

Most diagnostic tests break down different personality types or styles into four main groups. Some, such as Myers-Briggs, divide the types even further, but groupings of four are basic enough to easily grasp, yet substantive enough to contain useful information.

When I'm working with clients on determining their styles, I use an online assessment called the Neethling Brain Instrument (NBI™) that breaks things down into eight dimensions. You can take the full assessment by going to www.11lawsoflikability.com/assessment. Enter the code "BOOK11" to receive a discount on the assessment.

However, everyone can get a general sense of basic style types by answering a few questions and applying the answers to a four-part matrix. One axis of the matrix represents how you make decisions, and the other represents what influences those decisions. Your natural tendencies—objective thinker or subjective thinker, rapid responder or considered responder—determine the category you fall within: Straight Line, Zig Zag, Angle, or Circle.

LIVE THE LAW: *UNDERSTAND YOU—*
PLOT YOUR STYLE

Figure out where you fall in the style matrix by charting your natural inclinations. You may not exactly match each aspect of a trait description. In each pair of traits, just choose the one that most closely describes you.

1. How do you make decisions and contribute to conversations?

FAST. You are decisive, quick to share your opinions, and animated during discussions, contributing frequently and using large gestures to express yourself. You tend to speak quickly and be direct.

CONSIDERED. You think about your options before settling on your opinion; you listen to other people's input before offering your thoughts; you are more reserved in your gestures and facial expressions than many of your colleagues. You speak in a deliberate way and choose your words carefully.

2. What influences your decisions, and what's your comfort level with self-disclosure?

OBJECTIVE. You focus on facts and figures, historical data, and quantifiable information. You tend to take a systematic approach to problem solving and hone in on details and specifics. You are less likely to share personal information about yourself than many of your colleagues, and you are less comfortable sharing your emotions.

SUBJECTIVE. You make decisions by tuning into what other people think about the situation, what the group energy is like, and what your gut intuition is telling you. You tend to generalize information and look at the big picture. You are open with your feelings and comfortable with emotion.

Plot your preferences in the style matrix, shown in Table 3-1, to determine if you are a Straight Line, a Zig Zag, an Angle, or a Circle. Be aware that you have qualities of every style in you, and that the matrix is meant to help you determine your dominant communication style. Read about the priorities and preferences of the other styles as well, and see if you can come up with people you know who fit those styles. I bet some people come to mind quickly. Think about how the differing communication styles might impact how you interact with people who don't fall into your same category.

Of course, we all have tendencies that show up in other categories. I'm a Zig Zag, but my obsession with being punctual makes my husband kid me about my Angle-ish inclinations. The point of

Table 3-1. Style matrix.[1]

FAST	
OBJECTIVE	**SUBJECTIVE**
Straight Line	*Zig Zag*
Priority: Get it done	**Priority:** Get creative
Description: Logical, rational, pragmatic, focused, concrete	**Description:** Imaginative, visual, future focused, intuitive
Values: Performance, direct and concise communication	**Values:** Experimenting, taking risks, high energy
Misperceived As: Arrogant, bossy, think they are always right	**Misperceived As:** Idealistic, impractical, too talkative

CONSIDERED	
OBJECTIVE	**SUBJECTIVE**
Angle	*Circle*
Priority: Get it right	**Priority:** Get consensus
Description: Organized, detail-oriented, systematic, habitual, efficient	**Description:** Sociable, tolerant, empathetic, supportive, perceptive
Values: Punctuality, thoroughness, historical proof	**Values:** Loyalty, cohesion, consensus, relationships
Misperceived As: Rigid, uptight, boring	**Misperceived As:** Too nice, pushover, overly sensitive

the matrix isn't to determine your style in a monolithic, unequivocal way, but to point out your dominant type and general tendencies. Understanding your own style—and learning how to pick up on the styles of others—helps you manage how you are perceived as well as your perceptions of those around you.

Good connections aren't dependent on falling into the same style quadrant. Somewhat surprisingly, the best and most innovative collaborations are most likely to happen between people whose styles are diagonally opposite on the matrix. Because their approaches to problem solving are so different, they tend to balance one another well. For example, thinking-outside-the-box Zig Zags and detail-oriented Angles often complement one another. Likewise, deadline-driven Straight Lines and consensus-building Circles working together can be extremely productive. Opposite styles may have the most potential for conflict, but they can also have the most potential for results.

However, any mix of styles can connect well. The key is to reduce misperceptions by staying aware of style differences and using them as the basis for playing to one another's strengths, not augmenting weaknesses until they crowd out everything else and solidify into misperceptions. You can really develop an appreciation for other people whose styles are not the same as yours, especially when they may be able to do things you can't and, what's more, don't want to do, and vice versa. That's why working with people with differing styles can create powerful connections and collaborations.

By learning to pick up on the clues people give about their styles, you can better understand their priorities and what drives their actions. Then you can adjust your communication tactics so that as other people form their impressions of you, they are not jarred by clashing style differences but rather can see through any differences to the real you. Understanding where other people fall on the matrix also helps you cut through your own possible misconceptions of them.

By the same token, understanding where *you* fall on the style matrix helps you stay aware of the clues you are putting out there for other people to see. How do those actions impact how you are perceived? And are you creating the best impression of your authentic self?

LIVE THE LAW: *UNDERSTAND OTHERS—
LOOK FOR CLUES*

Once I was pitching a program on communication styles to the head of a New York City government agency, and in the middle of the conversation the director stopped and challenged me: "So what's my style?" he asked. I looked at him and looked around his office to confirm what I had already observed about him. There were plants and family photos throughout the office, indicating a nurturing Circle style, but he was wearing a purple shirt with a funky tie, and his papers were organized not in file drawers but in various slightly disheveled stacks on every flat surface in the room, demonstrating a dominant out-of-the-box Zig Zag approach. I told him I thought he was a Zig Zag, which is what he'd already determined he was, too. He hired me on the spot.

Simply by using our normal powers of observation, we can often identify a person's dominant style. Take this quiz to practice differentiating styles based on what you observe.

TEST YOUR ABILITY TO DIFFERENTIATE STYLES

Directions: For each description, choose the style that most closely matches it.

1. Whose office is this?
   a) There are plenty of comfy places to sit, a big assortment of pens on the desk, and lots of artwork on the walls.

b) Neat, labeled files are stacked in holders; there's a clean, well-organized desk; there's a staff kitchen where teas, coffees, and utensils are separated into clearly marked drawers.

c) Furnishings are spare but enough chairs are assembled for small groups to have discussions; walls are bare, save for the functional whiteboards marked with tasks, directives, and goals.

d) Bulletin boards are covered in colorful notes and inspirational paraphernalia; a cluttered desk has some sort of puzzle-type toy on it, and there's a basketball hoop on the back of the door.

2. Who is most likely to ask these questions?
   a) What's the first step? Do you have a plan? How do you want to approach the task?
   b) What's the goal? What are your resources? What is your deadline?
   c) Who is involved? Whom do I get to work with? How does the other team feel about this?
   d) Why are we doing it this way? Can you envision the process? Are you open to trying things differently?

3. Who would probably exhibit the following body language?
   a) These people make lots of expressive hand gestures, and are prone to perching on the edge of a table or sitting with one foot tucked beneath them.
   b) This person has animated facial expressions and a tendency to touch the other person's shoulder or arm when saying hello.
   c) This person frequently glances at the clock on the wall and often jiggles a leg or drums fingers on a table.

d) This person sits erectly in a chair and makes infrequent facial expressions, but eyes are alert and taking everything in.

4. Who would be wearing this suit?
   a) As attire, it's standard-issue blue, completely acceptable but not particularly distinct.
   b) It's carefully chosen, well tailored, and perfectly ironed and accessorized.
   c) Basic pieces are accented by a bright shirt or boldly patterned tie.
   d) Flattering but not flashy, a woman might complement this outfit with a favorite scarf; a man might accent the jacket with a tie his five-year-old gave him for Father's Day.

Answers:

1. a) Circle	b) Angle	c) Straight Line	d) Zig Zag
2. a) Angle	b) Straight Line	c) Circle	d) Zig Zag
3. a) Zig Zag	b) Circle	c) Straight Line	d) Angle
4. a) Straight Line	b) Angle	c) Zig Zag	d) Circle

Keep an Open Mind

One of the most powerful ways to reduce misperceptions that others might form of you is to stay open to how you are shaping your perceptions of them. If you rush to judgment about someone, chances are that person may have the same reaction to you. Monkey see, monkey do. If you don't want people to make assumptions about you that they automatically consider as facts, be aware of not falling into the same habit. In other words: *Stay unconvinced.*

It is natural for us to form first impressions when we meet someone. The challenge is to remain open to letting the other person change. All too often we jump to conclusions, but the next time you find yourself forming perceptions too quickly, stop and ask yourself, "How else can I interpret that person, that action, that situation?" People often act based on what they expect someone else's reaction to be. You can change the outcome of a situation by keeping an open mind and not pigeonholing other people into what you already believe about them. Lead by example, and let it be clear that your perceptions continue to take shape as your connection with someone progresses.

After Erica and I unexpectedly bonded during spring break, I thought back on how I'd acted toward her before our trip. I realized that since I had already decided she was a stuck-up rich girl, I probably hadn't acted very kindly toward her. In fact, if I was honest, I had treated her exactly the way I thought she was treating me, with thinly veiled contempt. And as my dad would have said, "The world is a mirror." What I got back was the same frostiness I was giving off. Had I remained open to other interpretations of her behavior, I could have had a great friend even sooner.

More recently I coached Liza, a new manager in her early thirties. She voluntarily shared her feelings with me about one of her colleagues, a woman named Drea, who was also a new manager as well as the mother of a toddler. Liza always felt that Drea was unfriendly. After a few attempts to chat with her, Liza concluded that Drea had no interest in being friendly, so she stopped making an effort.

One Saturday afternoon Liza ran into Drea in the town where they both lived, and they wound up sharing more during those fifteen minutes of chatting on the street than they had in the previous year they'd worked together. It turned out that Drea was having problems with her son and, consequently, feeling overwhelmed by work. That conversation broke the ice. Liza was able to appreciate the pressures Drea was under outside the office, pressures that contributed to her seeming closed and unapproachable, and Drea felt relieved to have her colleague understand her very taxing situation. The two women wound up not only becoming friends, but finding ways to collaborate at work, building on their new appreciations for one another, and becoming even more productive at work in the process.

You never know what else is going on in somebody's life. If you jump to conclusions about someone based on limited, pro-scribed interactions, you close the door to the possibility of deep-ening your connection. Whether with a new acquaintance or an existing relationship, stay open to the possibility that your per-ceptions aren't entirely accurate; it just may give you the oppor-tunity to strengthen a bond.

Inconsistent Communications

There are three components that contribute to the signals you send out to other people, and they are often referred to by trainers as the three Vs of communication: verbal (the words you choose), vocal (the tone and animation in your voice), and visual (your fa-cial expressions and body language). The key to transmitting the true you is to be consistent verbally, vocally, and visually when communicating. If not, other people will pick up on your mixed messages and perceive you as being inauthentic or confused.

I was once hired by a top financial services firm to conduct workshops with senior executives about the employee recruitment process. One of the executives, a middle-aged man named Gary, was perhaps the most extreme example of an inconsistent commu-nicator I've yet come across. Part of our work involved role-playing final interviews, during which the executive was to express the very real benefits and appeal of working for the company. When Gary and I sat down for the mock interview, he started his spiel in a monotone drone, telling me what a great company it was to work for, rarely making eye contact with me, and acting as if he was reciting a script. It was unbelievable. *He* was unbelievable, because he was being completely inconsistent in what he was communicating. If it had been an actual situation, and I had been the candidate listening to him offer me the position, there's no way I would have been convinced by him to accept the offer.

It's All in Your Body

My mother always told me, "It's not what you say, but how you say it." Her words immediately leaped to mind when I came across the work of psychologist Albert Mehrabian. He's done extensive research to determine how, in a face-to-face setting, someone is most likely to feel about you. In his book *Silent Messages*, Mehrabian lays out a formula for the factors that constitute a person's "Total Liking."

7% Verbal Liking + 38% Vocal Liking + 55% Facial Liking[2]

In other words, what you say has very little meaning if your body isn't backing it up. Think about the average teenager who may say "Fine," with crossed arms and a gaze fixed on the ceiling. The unspoken message here is quite clearly, "No, it is *not* fine." When you meet someone for the first time and say, "It's so nice to meet you," do you typically use a warm tone of voice, smile, and look that person directly in the eye? Or are you more apt to shyly avert your gaze or speak in a clipped manner that indicates you're short on time? What are you visually communicating to the other person? Are your vocal (tone) and visual (facial and body) communications backing up your verbal message?

Decide what image you want to portray, then determine how to convey it. Your body language can divulge your disinterest or, conversely, it can affirm your attentiveness and confidence.

LIVE THE LAW: *USE WHAT YOUR MOMMA GAVE YOU*

After coaching thousands of students on interviewing techniques, I have come to realize that people are largely unaware of their natural body language. I often think about the first time I was videotaped for a practice interview, while still in business school: I was a curl twirler. While answering questions, my finger would be winding and unwinding a lock of hair—not exactly the professional image I wanted to project. Increasing your awareness about your body language is an effective way to improve it, ensuring that it's in sync with the verbal messages you want to transmit. Follow these steps:

1. **Learn More.** What are you communicating with your body language? The best way to find out is to watch yourself on video. If you already have footage, pull it out and watch it. Even a few minutes of video recorded on a smartphone will show you what you need to know. Are you smiley but slouchy? Alert but off-puttingly stern? Make note of the things you are naturally doing well and where you could use improvement. Do you laugh nervously? Play with your rings? Jingle something in your pocket? Even being marginally more conscious of the unspoken signals you are sending goes a long way, compelling you to stand straighter and maintain eye contact. If you don't have video footage of yourself to watch, just ask some people who know you well what your common fidgets and general mannerisms and body language are. They will be able to tell you!

2. **Pay Attention.** Watch the body language of those around you. What types of gestures, stances, and facial expressions do people exhibit? And what messages do these signals convey

to you? If you observe things that resonate with you in a positive way, try incorporating them into your own body-language repertoire. Expanding our abilities to communicate is all about skill development, and new skills need to be practiced before we can become comfortable with them.

3. **Pick and Choose.** The behaviors listed in Table 3-2 are common and powerful transmitters of nonverbal signals. Choose one or two where you have room for improvement, then practice the behavior.

Self-Doubt

A common reason our bodies and voices can often give us away is that we are feeling self-doubt. If you don't believe the message you are trying to transmit, why should anybody else?

In Chapter 2, we discussed the law of self-image and looked at how to connect with our best images of our authentic selves. Remember the advice about how to "choose your words"? Well, to project those best words that define you, you must believe them, and a crucial part of that is projecting through body language. The words you choose represent how you perceive yourself, and how you want others to perceive you. Apply the same techniques we used in Chapter 2 to ensure that other people's perceptions of you are in line with what you want to express.

Say Nice Things

When you are feeling good about yourself, your positive body language will fall into place. Before walking into a meeting or picking up the phone to make an important call, ask yourself, "What are the words on my list that I want to convey at this moment?" Think about what those words would look like in action, and hold

Table 3-2. Vocal and visual communication behaviors.

Eye Contact	To express interest and confidence, eye contact needs to be consistent. Practice in a mirror if you have to, looking yourself straight in the eye and imagining yourself talking to an important client or senior colleague. Maintain eye contact in a natural way. This doesn't mean staring, it means engaging. With positive, effective eye contact, there are breaks of usually two to five seconds that naturally happen between the periods of eye contact.
Pauses	Pauses are powerful. They can communicate thoughtfulness, confidence, and a natural comfort with your surroundings. To transition from pauses back into conversation, use phrases that remark on what the other person just said or seek to clarify it, if necessary: "I have never thought about that before" or "If I understand you correctly, you are saying. . . ."
Stance	Stand tall! A slouch or an overly relaxed stance reads as lacking assurance in yourself and interest in the other person. I'm only four feet ten, but when I imagine pulling up on a marionette string attached to the top of my head, everything straightens out. I can't tell you how many times someone has come over to me after one of my presentations and said, "Wow, you really are short!" They're always surprised to stand next to me and get a sense of my actual height because they say, "You come off as being taller."
Voice	Forcing yourself to sound unnaturally animated or enthusiastic can backfire. It comes off as insincere and fake. Improve your vocal signals by making sure your delivery sounds confident. Don't mumble or speak in a stilted fashion, resist the urge to use "ums" and "ahs," and don't end your sentences by raising your voice as if you're posing a question.

that image in your mind. Realize that you already know what it looks like to successfully transmit the positive message you intend. Forget about the bully on your shoulder; now is the time to champion the cheerleader.

The key is to think it first and feel it in your body, then let it happen. Authenticity comes from being true to the moment, in the moment. If you get yourself in a positive frame of mind, your body will follow.

Another way to build positive perceptions is by saying nice things to someone else. Spend some time noticing what you admire or appreciate about those around you and how those things positively impact your perceptions of those people, then tell them what you admire. The results are almost always win-win. Compliment a colleague on how he handled a sticky client situation, and you may also walk away with new insights about how to proceed in a difficult situation of your own. The act of putting our impressions into words helps us understand what informs the perceptions we make of other people, and how what we do shapes the perceptions others are making of us.

Even telling a stranger what you admire about her can have a positive impact. Complimenting that woman in front of you in the grocery store checkout line on her coat makes both of you feel good. Saying nice things to people we don't know can even yield more far-reaching results. My friend Bill likes to ride his bike to the gym, and for a time he kept noticing a beautiful bicycle that was often locked to the rack. One morning as he was leaving, the owner of the bike was there unlocking it. Bill went up to him and told him that he thought the man had the greatest bike he'd ever seen. They ended up chatting for a half-hour and realized that they had all sorts of things in common. The guy was a law professor at the nearby university where Bill had received his marketing degree. The two became friends and not only started biking together but also, on several occasions, recommended clients to one another.

Communicating what we appreciate by saying nice things has powerful results for ourselves and those around us. Opening up a conversation can be opening up a world of new possibilities.

Use Positive Framing

Imagine that you have two direct reports and you ask each of them how things went on a task they've just completed. One answers, "It didn't go nearly as badly as the last time; that last one was a disaster." The other says, "I learned a lot from the last experience and this time it went much more smoothly." The content of their responses is not significantly different, but which one has the more positive impact on your perceptions of the employee? The second one, of course. Emphasizing the negative creates a negative impression; emphasizing the positive puts the speaker in a positive light.

In Chapter 2 you learned how *external framing* can be used to project your positive self-perceptions. The same principle holds true when it comes to affecting the perceptions others have of you. Word choice is a powerful tool for shaping the impressions you want to create. Remember the rules for effective external framing from the last chapter.

- Start with the positive.
- Choose strong actionable verbs.
- Focus on what you *can* do.
- Translate mistakes into knowledge and opportunity.

If you minimize your accomplishments, that's what people will believe about you. If you emphasize your accomplishments, that is how you will be perceived. Use the word "I" when applicable, and give other people their due as well. Self-acknowledgment doesn't need to come across as bragging, and if you do it in an authentic way, it won't.

Fake It Till You Make It Real

Take the lessons you've learned about improving your body language and put them into practice. Stand tall, make direct eye contact, and remember to smile. Even if you've still got the training wheels on, once you start presenting the image of yourself that you want others to have, you'll see that it has a powerful impact. If you seem to believe in yourself, others will too.

When I walked into the office of the head of training at JPMorgan Chase, I entered with confidence, as though I were accustomed to holding these meetings, even though it was the first time I was attempting to sell my not-yet-formed company's services. But I had been in plenty of client meetings during my tenure at the financial services firm where I previously worked. Thinking back on those experiences helped remind me what comfortable looks and feels like. By tapping into my memories of these similar situations, I leveraged that past experience to instruct myself how to *act as if*. And I landed the client. How I perceived of myself was how the client perceived of me.

Work from the Outside In

Just as what you wear affects how you feel about yourself, it also has a dramatic impact on how others see you. I remember teaching a weeklong seminar, and when I walked into the room on the first morning there was a woman wrapped in a thick black jacket hunched over one of the tables. The way she held herself, hidden in that dark coat, with something of a scowl on her face, made me assume that she would be cold and reticent. But when I turned to start the session I saw that she had taken off her coat, and underneath was a bright orange top. The vibrant color brought a huge smile to my face, which is what she saw when I greeted her, and she beamed right back.

If she had still been wrapped in the thick, dark jacket, I'm sure

BODY LANGUAGE—SOMETIMES IT DOESN'T TRANSLATE!

When dealing with international clients or partners, remember that different cultures have different codes of propriety and conduct that are often expressed in nonverbal ways. During my first business trip to Japan, I was surprised to discover that a firm handshake and confident eye contact were not the normal methods for greeting colleagues. The Japanese place a high premium on respect and deference, so approaching a superior as you would a peer is strictly taboo. Instead, Japanese employees greet senior colleagues—even, as I found out, if they're foreign—with a nod and a bow, eyes downcast. Looking me in the eye would have been unspeakably rude, and it's imperative that the junior employee bow more deeply than the senior employee, to show respect. This had hilarious results for one of my American colleagues, who spent a good five minutes repeatedly bowing with a junior employee in a Japanese firm, until he realized that he needed to let the Japanese businessman bow more deeply so that the businessman could show his deference to his American guest.

A healthy amount of in-the-moment awareness is all it usually takes to pick up on these signals and act accordingly. Insensitive gaffes, though, can have big consequences. One colleague told me about a meeting he'd been in with several of his firm's employees and their Japanese clients. As was customary for the Japanese, the group had respectfully exchanged business cards, presenting the cards with both hands, the information on the card facing the recipient. During the meeting, though, one of the firm's junior employees absentmindedly picked up one of the senior Japanese businessperson's cards and, while mulling something over, started tapping it on his mouth until it was finally between his lips. The Japanese clients were extremely offended and no longer wanted to deal with that employee.

our initial encounter would have been more formal, because I would have been approaching her with the less-than-welcoming first impression I'd formed based on her attire, hunched body language, and scowl. Instead the sunshiny hue of her top instantly changed my perception of her, and we were able to connect with one another's warmth immediately.

Be You, Be Aware, Be Flexible

The power in understanding how our actions create others' perceptions of us is that we gain significant control over creating those perceptions. Be comfortable being you in a situation, and be aware of the signals you are picking up from others. Use your knowledge about styles to stay flexible and moderate your behavior to the best effect. If you're a Zig Zag and approach problem solving "from all sides at once," but you are working with a Straight Line who is focused on achieving the most direct results, rein in some of your Zig Zagging to increase the effectiveness of the collaboration and convey that you can adapt to different situations as needed.

Flexing your style isn't about imitating another person or suppressing your impulses. It is about fine-tuning your messages to communicate effectively and enable others to perceive the true you.

Refresh Your Memory

The Law of Perception. Perception is reality. How you perceive others is your reality about them, and the same is true for them of you.

The Sublaw of First Impressions. It is much easier to make a good first impression than to change a bad one. Do it right the first time.

We Create Our Perceptions. Just as we create first impressions, we create perceptions based on them. Be your authentic self to transmit the real you to others and impact their perceptions of you.

Study the Style Matrix. Learn your dominant communication style and observe the styles of those around you, to create effective perceptions and avoid misperceptions.

Keep an Open Mind. Stay open to changing your perceptions of people as your connections with them grow. That way you'll also increase the likelihood that they'll stay open to changing their perception of you.

Be Consistent. To positively communicate your authentic self, make sure all your modes of messaging—verbal, vocal, and visual—are in sync.

Do Away with Self-Doubt. To connect with your best perceptions of yourself, and convey those perceptions to others, harness the strategies of saying nice things, using positive reframing, faking it till you make it real, and working from the outside in.

Be Flexible. Be aware of the signals you are putting out there and the ones other people are transmitting to you, and modify your behavior when necessary to ensure you are being perceived in the most authentic way.

4

The Law of Energy

"Our energy is in proportion to the resistance it meets."
— William Hazlitt, seventeenth-century essayist

A few years ago I was hired by Rick, the director of under-
graduate career counseling at a university, to conduct a
series of workshops about interviewing skills. At the end of
one of the sessions we went back to his office to chat about
the immediate student feedback, which had been extremely
enthusiastic. A former student who took my workshop the year
before had joined me in my presentation to share how he had
put the techniques he'd learned into action and landed his
first-choice job. Rick and I were both beaming as we discussed how the students seemed to be incorporating the
skills we were teaching them.

Then we had to wrap up our conversation because Rick
had a one-on-one meeting scheduled with a student. At that
point, I observed a distinct change in Rick's energy. The smile
disappeared, his body seemed to tense up, and his demeanor became distracted. I wondered if I had said or done
something to upset him, and asked him. It turned out that the

meeting he was about to have was with a student who, in his words, drove him crazy.

The student had been scheduling meetings with him practically every week, showing up to their sessions a fuming ball of energy. The student would rapidly detail all the contact he'd had with recruiters since their last session, and whenever he didn't hear back from a recruiter he would vehemently denounce Rick's advice. Rick knew that it was his job to help the student, and wanted to do so, but the student's aggressive, offensive attitude put Rick on the defense. Rick found it difficult to deal with the student in an instructive way. As Rick told me about this situation he got completely worked up, talking more rapidly and sitting forward in his chair in an agitated way.

"I'm dreading the appointment," he told me. "I always feel so frustrated and useless after meeting with this student, and he walks into my office with such an attitude."

I listened attentively, indicating that I could empathize with the dread he was feeling about the upcoming meeting. Then I said to him, "Let's try something. Tell me about a student you really like." Rick told me about another student he was working with one-on-one, but this student he found to be dynamic, proactive, and engaging. In fact, Rick was able to successfully connect the student with an important recruiter. As he told me this story, his tone of voice became lighter, his body relaxed, and suddenly he was smiling again.

"Okay," I said, "I want you to keep this second student in mind, the one you really admire, until the problematic student walks in the door. See if you get a different response from him than what you are used to." He agreed to give it a try.

Later that afternoon, Rick called me. "That was so great!" he said. "It totally worked! I had a completely different kind of interaction, and our meeting was positive and productive." He couldn't get the words out fast enough.

Whenever we saw one another, Rick kept me posted about his progress with this student. Future interactions between the two of them continued getting better, and eventually he came to not only understand and more effectively assist the student, but to like him as well.

During any interaction, each person involved transmits energy that affects the dynamic of that relationship. Becoming more conscious of how we are acting and feeling, how the other person is acting and feeling, and what that combination contributes to our encounters is a powerful tool for harnessing likability and building meaningful connections. Often we are not even aware of the energy we ourselves are giving off. Energy impacts our communication, and it can either work for us or against us.

Energy Is Contagious

Think about a recent situation that went well for you. If you had to describe your mood during that moment and your approach to the situation, what would you say? Whatever words you use, describe the vibe you were giving off and the energy you were putting out. Your description should encapsulate the feeling the other person or people were getting from you, perhaps even before you said a word.

Sometimes people might even sum up their natural energy and approach to life as a motto: "Never let them see you sweat," or "You're never fully dressed without a smile." These are their words to live by, and they can encapsulate energy in a distilled, tangible way. Energy is derived from both your natural personality and your actual mood in a moment. You can feel your own energy in your body, your face, your stance, even in the way you are breathing. Other people pick up on these signals and on the words you choose in a given moment. Likewise, you pick up on the energy of others and respond to it in kind.

The kind of energy we bring to a situation impacts the ways our interactions with the world unfold. Energy is contagious—that is the *law of energy*. Our own output of energy can energize other people or deflate them, contribute to productivity or add to the confusion. Energy affects the course of interactions and facilitates connections.

Your energy during an interaction will be picked up on by others and influence the outcome. What you give off is what you get back, so getting your energy to an optimal place before entering a situation can make all the difference. The key is to enable the energy that is going to best serve the situation. When we understand that energy is something we create, we can work on driving the energy rather than having it drive us. In other words, know what energy is most useful to bring to a given situation or when dealing with a specific person, and get yourself to that optimal place so that you can better influence the outcome.

Finding Energy That Works

To be perceived as authentic and sincere, you must be true to yourself and your energy in a situation. The key isn't to artificially be the peppiest person in the room. It's far more important to be sincere. But this doesn't mean letting a bad day ride roughshod over you and the energy you are putting out to others either. We can put forth positive energy that is sincere, even when faced with challenges, difficulties, or distractions. This is a fundamental part of connecting effectively. Learning how to put out the right energy at the right time in the right place—and doing it authentically—is a fundamental part of effectively connecting with others. Authentic positive energy is likable.

To understand how the law of energy works, consider three questions:

1. Where is your energy right now?
2. Where is the other person's energy?
3. What energy knowledge do you possess about yourself, and about the energy expectations that exist between you and the other person?

You First: Where Is Your Energy Right Now?

To harness our energy to the best effect, we must be in tune with it. That means knowing what vibe we are giving off at any given moment, determining how well it is working, and if necessary, adjusting it.

Rick was completely unaware that he was helping to create unpleasant interactions with his aggressive student. By approaching those meetings with dread—which, as I saw firsthand, he was clearly indicating with his body language and tone of voice—he was transmitting a negative vibe to his student. The fact that their sessions were difficult was a self-fulfilling prophecy. Once Rick adjusted his approach and brought a more open and positive energy to their sessions, he was able to start successfully connecting with the student. The student picked up on Rick's positive vibe, became less combative, and was able to accomplish some truly productive work.

As Albert Einstein said, "Insanity is doing the same thing over and over again and expecting different results." Assess your output of energy in a situation and, if you see that it could be improved, don't be afraid to change it. If necessary, you can tap into memories of other times you've naturally exuded positive energy and harness these recollections to adjust your approach to a new situation or person. Remember, too, that it is sometimes necessary to lead by example. Depending on the energy that other people are bringing to the interaction, it may take them a while to respond to your shift, but by taking action and making adjustments, you are making the first step in bringing around more positive results.

LIVE THE LAW: *SHIFT YOUR ENERGY*

When entering a situation where you don't feel as if you are putting your best foot forward, shift your energy to let the positive, authentic you come through.

Think about the emotion you want to embody and then conjure up a memory of a very specific time when you felt that way. Recall as many details as you can to make the memory as strong as possible: Hear the client comment on the effectiveness of your solution, see the look of admiration from your colleagues, remember what it felt like to accomplish that monumental task on time and on budget. What happens? If you practice this simple technique, you will find that your body relaxes, you feel more naturally confident, and your energy shifts toward the memory energy—that positive energy—you are reconnecting with. Carry this energy shift with you into the new situation and that is the energy you'll give off.

Next, Them: Where Is the Other Person's Energy?

A connection is something that, by virtue of what it is, requires two people. To impact the energy of a situation in the most positive way, we need to be aware not only of our energy signals, but the other person's energy signals, too.

There are many times when we already instinctively do this. When we call someone and the person answers with a "Hello," we immediately interpret the energy on the other end of the line through this single word and the way it was delivered. Was it curt, chipper, or guarded?

Body language, tone of voice, and rate of speech are all indicators of someone's energy. Someone who is making sweeping arm gestures and talking a mile a minute in a scattered way gives off a completely different vibe than someone who is speaking calmly and reflectively with arms crossed in a manner that indicates careful contemplation.

Be open to the fact that your interpretations of energy signals might need more clarity to be fully accurate. Downcast eyes and crossed arms might indicate that someone is uninterested or bored, but, in a different context, those gestures might just mean that the person is giving the matter further thought. If you are unsure of the messages someone is sending, ask questions to gain clarity. Be aware of your timing and tone when making such inquiries, and use neutral language. You can broach your desire for clarification with such phrases as:

- Would it help to talk through anything?
- What else is on your mind?
- What do you think about that?
- Is everything okay?

Energy Has Power

In addition to harnessing your own energy, understanding the energy that others bring to a situation is vital to impacting the overall shape of the encounter—and its outcome.

The most powerful experience I've had, to date, happened while conducting a seminar in conflict resolution at a government agency where employees of many different ethnicities worked. In the morning we focused on the best language to use when addressing workplace conflicts, the different approaches that can be taken to resolve conflicts, and how to improve communication. At the end of the day, I paired off the staff members to discuss and verbalize real workplace conflicts.

One woman told her partner that she'd overheard one of their coworkers, an Irish-American woman, say about a client, "My word, why can't people just speak English?" The comment had really hurt the woman who was relating the anecdote. She herself was Latina and she'd taken the comment as a personal affront. She told her partner that after this happened, she found it difficult to work next to the woman or even speak to her, and in truth hadn't spoken one word to her since the incident.

I asked this woman if we could share the conflict with the group. She agreed, and so I asked her to relay the story to everyone. As she did so, her words, tone of voice, and body language all expressed the very strong anger she felt about the situation. Immediately I could feel the rest of the group picking up on it. "You're kidding me!" one woman shouted. "That's completely unacceptable!" a man barked from the back of the room. With what felt like the flick of a switch, the group energy had become aggressive and hostile, and it just kept intensifying. It felt as if a mob mentality had suddenly taken over the room.

"Okay, hold on for a second," I said. "Is it possible that this comment was taken out of context? Do you know the full extent of the client case history? Or what the exact exchange between the client and the worker was?" The group appeared willing to listen, so I continued. "Let's think for a moment about what else may have motivated this coworker's comment." As the group began to discuss the different possibilities, the vibe in the room changed. Someone suggested that maybe the woman was frustrated by her inability to do her job. Another person suggested that perhaps the woman was afraid of losing her job because she was not bilingual. The Latina woman who'd originally related the anecdote even ventured that by not trying to understand the full context of the situation before taking offense at it, perhaps she had helped perpetuate the hostile work environment that she was complaining about. By the end of the session, the aggressive energy had dissipated and evolved into curiosity and even sympathy. By probing the situation and relinquishing fixed, rigid assumptions, the group was able to change its energy from negative to at least neutral and open, clearing the way to resolve the conflict in the most constructive way.

Understanding the energy of a person or a group of people enables us to more productively connect with them. In the end, it is not about isolated individuals, but about how those individuals share their energies to interact, understand one another, and connect.

LIVE THE LAW: *MEET THEM WHERE THEY ARE*

When you are faced with difficult, challenging, or unproductive energy from someone else, you have four options:

1. **Add Fuel to the Fire.** Often this is the reaction that feels easiest and most instinctual, because you impulsively let loose with exactly what you are thinking and feeling. But this kind of reaction also demonstrates a lack of deeper understanding about the person or situation at hand. By simply returning someone else's negative or destructive energy, you exacerbate and amplify it. That's not a good outcome.

2. **Brush Them Off.** Imagine a coworker coming into a meeting, riled up about something. She's worked herself into a state, and your response is, "Just calm down, I'm sure everything will be fine." Such a response may seem well intentioned—after all, you are just trying to counter or shift what you see as unhelpful or unproductive energy—but it typically backfires, because it ignores and invalidates the coworker's current frame of mind and can leave her feeling misunderstood. Again, not good.

3. **Extract Yourself.** This can be an effective method, as long as you are harnessing it in a positive way. Sometimes extracting yourself from a difficult situation can indicate that you are burying your head in the sand, avoiding it in the hopes that it will just go away. This can leave the other person feeling ignored, continuing the adverse energy. But if you realize that contributing your current energy isn't going to help the situation, extracting yourself can give you the chance to shift your approach and come back to the situation in a productive way. This option may also give the other person time to get into a better frame of mind and reengage the situation with constructive energy.

4. **Meet Them Where They Are—Almost.** This is by far the most effective way to help shift someone else's energy so that you can better connect. When dealing with other people, read the signals they are sending out; listen to what they are saying and validate their energy state by responding with energy that is just below or just above what they are expressing. Matching their energy exactly will not help them shift out of a negative state, but *almost* matching it will let them know you understand what they are saying, and it will give them options for adjusting their energy positively. The response to the riled-up coworker isn't, "Relax, it will be fine," but "Oh, I can't believe that happened!" or "I can see that you're really upset by that." Don't counter the coworker's frustration by playing it down. Instead, meet the coworker's energy close to where it is, then gradually lift the mood at a natural pace, helping him shift his energy and settle into a more moderate, open frame of mind.

Helping other people make an energy shift increases our chances of connecting with them and building a meaningful relationship. It also increases trust and creates "mood memory," a concept we'll take a closer look at in Chapter 8.

Let's imagine one scenario with three possible outcomes. Let's say there is a couple, Sheila and Charles, on their way to an event. Sheila is driving and she's gotten rather lost, which makes her anxious that they'll be late. As she gets more and more turned around she gets more and more upset, frantically expressing that she doesn't know what to do. She *hates* being late.

Charles, sitting in the passenger seat, knows Sheila hates to be late. In the first possible outcome, he meets Sheila's panic with anger and shouting. Now, not only are they lost and running late, but they're also in a fight. Charles exacerbated Sheila's panic by reacting to the moment's negative energy with more negative energy, feeding it back to Sheila until the situation is spinning out of control.

In the second possible outcome, Charles responds to Sheila's panic with a casual "Calm down, it's no big deal. Who cares if we're late?" Clearly Sheila cares if they're late, even if Charles doesn't, and she interprets Charles's nonchalance as him not listening to and understanding what she is saying. She may even read more into it, hearing the unspoken message in his words that her reaction is unreasonable and irrational. She gets even more upset.

In the third possible outcome, Charles says to Sheila, in a concerned tone, "I know you hate being late." Then, in a slightly more relaxed tone, but still sounding attentive, he says, "Okay, we have about fifteen minutes to get there. Should we call and let them know we're lost? Maybe they can give us directions." Now he's trying to meet Sheila close to where she is and help her shift away from her panic to a mindset that is better for her and the situation. Charles is demonstrating that he is concerned, interested, and understands Sheila's problem, and his energy matches hers in seriousness but is several notches more calm. He is not flat-out taking control in a way that would further set her off, but rather posing a question to create constructive energy so that they can both participate in solving the problem.

I call this third response *suggestive* or *probing questioning*. The key is to remember that you might not get the answer you are hoping for, and you have to be all right with that. Otherwise, you are not truly asking a question but rather issuing a statement with a question mark attached to it, and this doesn't keep the situation open to mutual resolution. If you don't get the answer you hoped you would, consider what else might be useful for the situation and try another tack.

The previous example is a social situation, but the same principles hold true in the business world. Mood and energy levels can shift positively or negatively depending on the actions and reactions of colleagues. A young colleague of mine, who was a few weeks into her new job, became upset that certain recruiting promises weren't being kept. She expressed her displeasure to an equally junior coworker, and he responded with a shock and outrage that matched her own. Feeding on that energy being reflected directly back at her, the woman marched over to HR and complained.

As it turns out, the recruiting promises were going to be kept, but the woman was so new on the job that she didn't yet understand the company's procedures. Luckily the situation blew over, though she of course deeply regretted filing the complaint, and even more deeply regretted having shared her dismay with that particular coworker. It immediately altered the course of their relationship, based on the woman's newly gathered *energy knowledge*.

Building Context: What Energy Knowledge Do You Possess?

Energy knowledge is what you know about your own energy, and what you know about the energy that exists between you and another person, based on past experiences. Being aware of our energy knowledge is key. This awareness allows us to project the energy we want others to see, communicate effectively in day-to-day situations, and adjust our energy under special circumstances to affect the most positive outcomes. Knowledge is power, and energy knowledge is no exception.

Your Energy Knowledge of You

We all have an energy persona. This persona is driven by our natural personality and general outlook on life—how we tend to view and react to different situations. What do you already know about your own energy? And are you aware of how other people read it? Even when the energy we are transmitting is good, it is important to understand what it is, and to adjust it at times to achieve varying results. "Good" energy doesn't necessarily mean "happy." Rather, it means whatever is productive and authentic for the situation and for you in that situation.

My friend Mary is a reporter by profession and naturally inquisitive, often asking lots of questions about what's going on in her friends' lives when they get together. But she noticed that frequently her friends didn't ask questions of her in return. Her energy persona was one of natural, perhaps constant, curiosity, and it was apparent to her friends, but to build the friendships in a way that opened up avenues for more give-and-take, Mary had to consciously adjust her natural tendency to ask questions and insert her own experiences at the right moments during these conversations. Sure, there were one or two friends who were too self-absorbed to pick up on Mary's effort to adjust her energy, but most of her friends, whether consciously or not, noticed and began talking to Mary about what was going on in her own life.

One of my clients, a woman named Carrie, has a gregarious personality and radiates a "you can lean on me" vibe. She is proud of being there for her friends when they are going through something difficult, and she is often the one to call and check in on them when the chips are down. Then she went through her own difficult time and was deeply dismayed to find that her phone didn't ring. People weren't checking in on her the way she did with them. She approached her closest friends to find out why and was shocked by their responses. "It doesn't seem like you want help," one of them said to her, and another said, "You seem so strong, you never seem to need anyone's help." Her competent, tough-girl energy made her friends think that she didn't want or need help, when exactly the opposite was true. By letting down her guard and toning down her ultra-strong vibe, shifting her energy to become more vulnerable with friends, she was able to get the support she needed and that her friends actually wanted to give her.

Understanding our own energy lets us know when it's working for us and when it's working against us. Adjustments to that energy at critical times can alter the energy of a given situation, making it more productive and fulfilling for all involved, increasing likability and the opportunities for connections.

LIVE THE LAW: *WHAT'S YOUR ENERGY?*

To get a better grasp on what your natural energy is, it's quite simple: Ask people. Choose at least five people, from different aspects of your life, and pick people with whom you have a well-established history. The more people you ask, the better. Start with these questions:

- How do you expect me to react when you are mad? When you're happy? When you're sad?

- In general, how would you describe my mood?

- How would you describe my personality?

- How would you say I respond when things get tough?

- What kind of friend/coworker am I?

Write down their responses and look for the descriptive words that appear again and again. Scrutinize your findings to see if there are differences between work, family, and friend descriptions. Sometimes the energy we emit can vary based on environment, and yet all these different energies can be authentic to us.

Your Energy Knowledge of Others

As soon as we meet people for the first time, we begin building our energy knowledge about them. If you have an established relationship with someone, ask yourself: What energy knowledge exists between us? When dealing with the energy between two people, it is important to manage expectations. I call these "energy expectations." Why does someone seek you out in a particular situation, and what makes you turn to certain other people? These choices are based on the energy knowledge we have of one another, so they are our energy expectations. Who do you approach when trying to figure out how to handle a situation with a coworker? Who is the first person you turn to when you want help solving a problem in an out-of-the-box way? Who do you seek out when you need to take a break and are looking for some fun or casual banter?

By understanding our energy expectations of other people, we can be clear about what we are looking for and communicate our need to them. Energy knowledge reduces miscommunications and frustrations. Although energy knowledge and energy expectations are valuable tools in deepening connections and attaining positive results, understand that there is always the possibility our expectations in a given situation won't be met. Don't use those moments to discard the energy knowledge you've accrued, but adjust your thinking so that you can determine if there is someone else you can approach to achieve your desired results. Stay open, too, to the possibility that your energy expectations may at times miss the mark and need to be reassessed.

Likewise, it is extremely useful to be aware of other people's energy expectations of us. This helps us more effectively accomplish what is expected of us. This knowledge can also help us decide when to consciously *not* fulfill those expectations if doing so would be detrimental.

As an example, a good friend of mine, Bryan, shared this story about an encounter with his coworker, Jay, who came to him complaining about their boss. Jay groused about how the boss wouldn't sign off on a project, even though Jay had reworked it what seemed countless times. In the past, Jay had sought Bryan's support and wanted him to take his side when he butted heads with the boss. Bryan knew that this was Jay's energy expectation of him, but he also knew that it wasn't going to help the situation any to fulfill that expectation. Bryan simply asked him, "Do you just want to vent, or do you want my advice?" He gave Jay those two options, essentially asking Jay how he wanted to proceed, but without giving any indication that he'd join Jay in bad-mouthing the boss.

When faced with only those options, Jay asked for Bryan's advice. Bryan told him that he understood how frustrating the situation must be, but that maybe what Jay needed instead was a debriefing about the project with the boss, to cohesively assess trouble spots, rather than reflexively responding to criticism in increments. Jay did eventually complete the project, and Bryan had helped him by *not* fulfilling the immediate energy expectations.

What we want—that is, our energy expectations—may not be what gets us a desired result. In other words, people are not always looking for productive energy. There is no sure-fire way to deal with this possibility. Ask yourself, what would help at that moment? And what would help in the long run? If it would help, ask the other person these questions too. Seek to strike a balance between what they want and what might actually serve them best.

If you give in to unproductive or destructive energy expectations, could it possibly harm the relationship or adversely affect the situation?

Our authentic energy is generally a consistent thing, but there are always moments when it may be adversely influenced by internal or external forces. This doesn't negate the energy knowledge we've accumulated, but rather reminds us how to harness what we know about energy to create positive outcomes even in challenging situations.

LIVE THE LAW: *DOES IT SERVE?*

Energy is the unspoken element present in any exchange, so it is important to be aware of the energy you are bringing with you to the interaction. Does your energy serve you, the situation, and the relationship? How is the other person's energy affecting those things?

Often we find ourselves experiencing a recurring negative response to someone else's energy. To better understand this, ask yourself:

- What am I getting from this shared energy experience?

- What is the other person possibly getting from it?

- What are the results?

- How could I change my reaction?

My client Aggie, a mid-level executive in her sixties, was an empty-nester and a recent divorcée. She'd begun taking every office interaction, large or small, as a personal offense. When she asked herself these very questions, she got some revelations:

- She was using anger to protect herself because it felt safer than vulnerability. She was also releasing anger in the workplace that she'd never expressed to her ex-husband.

- Her negative energy resulted in her feeling isolated from her coworkers in both personal and professional ways.

- If she stopped assuming that everyone was suddenly out to get her, she'd be able to bring less anger to her interactions and a more neutral energy, which would build understanding, inclusion, and productivity.

If you ask yourself the same questions and discover your energy doesn't serve a situation, adjust it by once again reviewing the exercise earlier in this chapter (see Live the Law: Shift Your Energy). Also, take a close look at your answer to one question in particular—How could I change my reaction?—to assess the energy shift you want to make. If another person's energy isn't serving the situation, build new energy knowledge with that person by helping her shift her energy in a more positive direction.

The Networking Application: Another Kind of Energy

Some people have a visceral negative response to the word *networking*. Others relish it, and some of us, well, our reaction depends on our energy at that moment and what we anticipate of the situation.

Use your energy knowledge of yourself to determine your *networking energy*. Under what circumstances does your best authentic energy come through? For instance, do you have the most natural positive energy during lunch or dinner situations, where you talk in a focused way with one or two people at your table? Or is your natural energy best at events such as cocktail receptions, where there is the opportunity to have brief interactions with many different people? Do you connect most positively with others at daytime events, or at those that happen after working hours?

Our energy ebbs and flows with different situations, locations, atmospheres, and times of day. Once we understand our networking energy, we can use it to create opportunities that align most fruitfully with how we naturally are. When you choose situations in which you are most comfortable—in other words, those that match your networking energy—your authentic self emerges.

Remember, though, that it's important to stretch yourself. This doesn't mean pretending to be comfortable when you're not, but rather actively shifting your energy in certain situations to broaden the scope and depth of your interactions. If your energy persona is naturally boisterous and you find that you are often at the center of conversations in networking situations, you may want to show that you can also be a good listener. If you more naturally assume a thoughtful, measured approach, look for opportunities to display how you can drive conversations too. By expanding the limits of when and how we can emit our authentic energy, we increase our potential for making and building meaningful connections.

Refresh Your Memory

The Law of Energy. Energy is contagious. What we give off is what we get back.

Find the Right Energy. Channeling your authentic energy doesn't mean constantly being happy. We can be genuine and real, and forge positive connections, even when faced with difficulties and challenges.

Identify Your Energy and Theirs. Recognizing your energy in a given situation helps you understand how you are contributing to the dynamic, and what you can change to effect the most positive outcome. Recognizing the energy others give off helps you adjust your own energy, if need be, to keep things on track.

Energy Knowledge Is Power. What we know about our own energy and the energy of others builds over time. This energy knowledge is a crucial part of deepening connections and increasing productivity. Energy expectations are what we expect from ourselves and others based on our energy knowledge.

Harness Your Networking Energy. Determining the situations in which you express your most positive authentic energy is the key to creating the most fruitful networking opportunities.

Part B

■

The Conversation: Always Have It

A few years ago I attended a round-table discussion in my industry and met Alana. She was seated at the other end of the table, so during the session we only exchanged eye contact, but after listening to her comments to the group I was curious to learn more about her. At the mingling session after the discussion, I sought out Alana to talk with her.

On the surface we didn't have much in common. She was considerably older than I was, probably in her sixties; she didn't have kids; she'd just moved to the area for the first time; and she had a niche specialty that I knew little about. And yet we effortlessly chatted until the event broke up. We decided to grab a quick glass of wine together, and two hours later we were still discovering all the things we connected on, and all the ways we might help one another. She had extensive experience as a coach, which she much preferred to being a trainer. The training component of my business was really taking off, and I loved that kind of work, so I needed to start finding collaborators who could fulfill my clients' coaching needs.

Today Alana and I are still working together, and we regularly refer clients to one another. Yet if I'd just gone on surface appearances when I met her, ignoring my curiosity about her and assuming that we had nothing in common, I never would have developed this fruitful relationship.

I remember walking home that night after Alana and I met, reiterating my philosophy to myself: *Always have the conversation.* My relationship with Alana is a continual reminder for me that when an opportunity to make a connection presents itself, take it. Engage someone in a conversation rather than staying silent, because you never know where that conversation may lead.

No matter where we are in our careers, forging new connections is a vital part of continued development and growth. When we are just starting out, creating and sustaining these connections can seem daunting. Once we've progressed in our professional lives, foundational skills such as effectively making new connections can atrophy, because we don't always use them as often as we once did. In either situation, meaningful relationships are the pathways to productive, fulfilling work, and the methods for building those relationships are the same: Be curious, listen, look for commonalities, and create positive feelings.

In the four chapters in this section, we'll take a closer look at these concepts to learn how to harness them effectively during moments of interaction, and to understand why you should *always* have the conversation.

5

The Law of Curiosity

"The important thing is not to stop questioning. Curiosity has its own reason for existing."

—Albert Einstein

Sylvia and I were standing in the same small group at a cocktail reception. We got to chatting for a few minutes, and when she heard that I was a coach, she mentioned that she was thinking about launching her own business. At this point her husband came to tell her that it was time for them to leave. She asked me if I'd like to grab coffee or lunch sometime and I said sure, as I almost always do in these situations. We exchanged business cards.

Sylvia followed up a few days later, suggesting some dates when we might have lunch. I had an extremely hectic schedule but found a pocket of time where I could wedge in a meeting. We finalized the details.

As I was walking down the street on my way to meet her, there were a million to-dos racing through my head, and I was wondering yet again what I'd been thinking when I agreed to the lunch date. I had barely spoken a few minutes to this woman so far, yet I'd prioritized our meeting over some important and time-sensitive tasks. Given my workload that week, having lunch with a virtual stranger was not exactly convenient.

When we sat down for lunch I suddenly realized that I barely knew anything about this woman, and that we didn't even have a natural starting point for conversation, so I just began asking her questions. Sylvia was also eager to hear more about my coaching work, and she was full of questions for me about my life and my projects. I'd assumed that she wanted to pick my brain about starting a business, so I sprinkled in advice as we spoke.

The more she told me about herself, the more curious I became. It turned out she was starting a virtual assistant business, worked at a private school, and conducted workshops for teenagers. It was all fascinating, and I wanted to know more about how she'd started the youth workshops initiative; more about the genesis of her virtual assistant business and the services she planned to offer; more about her successes organizing assembly programs for private schools.

The connections between us—and the opportunities for significantly helping one another—continued to unfold. I had no idea just how much there was to talk about until we started asking each other questions.

Curiosity may have killed the cat, but I can tell you it never killed a conversation. In fact, showing genuine curiosity about a person's job, life, interests, opinions, or needs is a great way to start a conversation, keep it going, and create connections.

Start by Being Curious

For many of us, starting a conversation with someone can be awkward. It can even feel like a chore. We may feel that we don't have anything interesting to offer the other person, or we don't want to embarrass ourselves by saying something dumb. Or maybe we simply feel as if we don't have time to meet someone new or to get to know someone better; after all, our lives are already too hectic and we don't feel as if we need any more friends. But continuing to initiate conversations and be curious about people is fundamental to building valuable relationships, because curiosity creates connections—that is the *law of curiosity*.

When you don't know how to start a conversation, start by being curious. And remember this: People love to talk. You just need to know how to get them going. I don't mean prompting them to launch into a monologue while you passively listen. A good conversation involves give-and-take; it's an exchange in which two people are genuinely engaged, listening, responding, and connecting to each other.

What would you genuinely like to know about the person? Are you wondering what it was like to lead that project that was such a smash hit? Have you heard stellar things about the person's racquetball game? If you are in a situation where you don't know anything at all about the person, ask general questions about the types of things you like to discover about people you meet—their hobbies, sports interests, favorite family or adventure vacation spots, or whatever else those things might be. Often picking one topic to pursue is all you need to get the dialogue rolling. Once you are talking, one subject can flow into the next one, which can flow into the next, and before you know it you've formed a connection.

Curiosity Creates Connections

Before meeting Sylvia for lunch, the only thing I really knew about her was that she hoped to expand a business venture she'd started, but I didn't even know what that venture was. I assumed that she'd asked me to lunch because she wanted some coaching around how to grow the business. As I continued asking her questions, seeking out how I might best be of assistance, I discovered more and more things that we had in common. I became intrigued by the evolution of her career and was especially excited to hear about her work with teens, an age group I'd been wanting to do more work with myself. Halfway through our salads it was no longer me coaching her, but her advising me on how to approach schools, when to book workshop programs with them, and what types of material worked best for that demographic. By the end of lunch, I'd hired her to consult with me on how to take the teen workshops I'd been designing and develop them into a full-fledged program.

Sylvia didn't come to the lunch expecting to be pitching her services, yet once she began to see how much our interests overlapped and how we could help one another, she became just as excited about it as I had. Our sincere curiosity about one another uncovered the myriad things we had in common. We'll see in Chapter 7 that the law of similarity—basically, what people have in common—can be one of the strongest connectors.

Without actively following our curiosity, Sylvia and I may not have so quickly uncovered the wealth of things we shared. As we worked together on my teen-workshops project, we didn't just discuss the task at hand, we talked about all the developments in each other's lives. I heard about her man troubles, she heard about my preschool quandaries, and we both helped each other think through our next steps. I wound up doing some coaching for her, too, consulting with her about how to grow her business. As a result of curiosity, we found multiple opportunities to work together, learned how many common interests we shared, and created a connection that outlasted not just the lunch but the launch of both our projects. We established a mutually rewarding relationship that continued to blossom.

Genuine curiosity can lead to more authentic, engaging conversations, which lay the foundation for sustained relationships. Even seasoned professionals who understand and have successfully built valuable connections over the years can benefit from remembering how to stay curious. As we get further along in our careers, our plates fill up and we can forget the value of nurturing new connections. Showing your genuine interest in someone else increases your likability, and you never know what opportunities it may open up.

Do You Know How to Ask a Question?

Curiosity seems simple enough—just start asking questions, right? That's one approach, but the success of it depends in part on how adept your conversation partner is at answering. You can help her along by varying the types of questions you pose. Ask open-ended questions at the start of a conversation, or when the conversation has hit a dead end. Use probing questions to further the dialogue when already immersed in a discussion. Choose broad topics or home in on something specific; it doesn't actually matter as long as what you are asking stokes your genuine curiosity about the person. Your goal is to uncover what you might have in common and what value you might bring to that person (the value aspect of our interactions with others is discussed further in Chapter 10).

Open Up and . . .

An open-ended question is simply one that requires more than a one- or two-word response. Typically, open-ended questions begin with *what, how, how come,* or *why.* Asking "What brings you here?" encourages the other person to provide a full response, whereas "Did your company send you?" only provides an opening for the other person to respond with a yes or no answer or possibly with the simple and conversation-limiting comeback, "Did yours?" Almost any question that can be answered with a yes or no or another one-word response can be rephrased to encourage a dialogue. Change the "Do you" or "Would you" into a "What" or a "How would you," and you've opened the door to a deeper conversation. "Do you like living in Atlanta?" becomes "What do you like about living in Atlanta?" "Would you recommend this vendor?" becomes "How has working with this vendor helped your company become more productive?"

When starting a conversation, try to have a few possible topics in mind, in case you need to go through a couple to get the conversation going. The openings you choose should be person- and situation-dependent, based on whom you're talking to and the circumstances that have brought you together. Do you work in the same industry? Are you both attending a specific event? Does the person live nearby? Making the openers relevant, even if only in a general way, creates context for the dialogue and fosters the connection that comes from it.

After you say "Hi, I am . . . ," test out some opening questions, as suggested here, and mix them up in different conversations to keep your communication and connection skills in optimal shape.

Make a Generic/Personal Inquiry

When you are meeting someone for the first time, especially if you are in an unfamiliar place, it can be difficult to find person- or situation-dependent openers. There are any number of broad fallback questions you can use in these situations, though, so put them to work. Many of these questions may seem like tired workhorses we've all heard before, so at first the person's responses might sound a bit rote or unenergetic. Nonetheless, you can use the responses to pick up on interesting details about the person so that you can then ask further questions and expand the conversation.

What do you do?

Although this one is trite, it's also tried and true. This is the ever-green question, something you can pose to anyone. A twist on this question is the equally reliable, "What do you do when you're not working?" If you are addressing someone who's retired or whose employment status is unknown or might be a delicate subject, you can tweak the question slightly by asking, "What field are you in?" or even "What do you want to do next?" The key when employing this question is to listen to and understand the answer; in other words, you need to truly hear what the person is saying. Try to glean what kind of client or contact information might be useful to the people you are speaking with through their responses, and follow up with new questions. How did they choose the industry they're in? If they are entrepreneurs, what was it like to land their first client? The possibilities for continuing the conversation are endless; just follow your curiosity. If someone in turn asks you, "What do you do?" take the opportunity to open up further avenues for dialogue. You can respond by saying, "For work or in my free time?"

What do you think of this (fill in the blank) weather?

Another standard icebreaker is to ask about the weather. A question about the stormy, unseasonably warm, or freezing cold weather may lead to meaningless small talk or it may open up more fruitful connections. The response could lead to a conversation about the cost of snow removal or comparisons with the weather in the person's hometown. It could lead to discussions about favorite vacation spots or why the weather is or isn't so great for your business. Start with a generic question and be ready to pursue further threads of dialogue based on responses.

Do you have kids?

This one can be a great conversation opener, even if the other person's answer is, "No." If the answer is "yes," then the abundance of possible topics is fairly clear. If the answer is "no," you can follow up with a lighthearted remark such as, "So you get to sleep through the night?" or "I miss the days of kid-free vacations," and see where that takes you.

Ask Their Opinion

Asking someone's opinion of something is a surefire conversation starter. Choose whatever topic you'd like—politics, sports, the latest news from Wall Street—just make sure it's something you want to talk about, too. If you are not genuinely curious about it you won't be fully engaged in the exchange, and your chance of forging a real connection diminishes.

As busy and seasoned professionals, sometimes we rush to get down to business. We would all benefit from remembering to stay curious and ask varied questions. Don't just stick to the usual. And be prepared to share your opinions as well—after all, you are trying to establish a dialogue. When pursuing the opinion route it's best to stay diplomatic with people you're still getting to know. Remember the advice every mother seems to dole out: "If you don't have anything nice to say, don't say anything at all." This doesn't mean you have to lie about what you think; what you *don't* say can speak volumes, too.

The options here are endless. Here are a few examples:

What did you think about that speaker?

This is an interesting option because it could so easily be a throwaway, not just for the person being addressed, but for you. Before you ask someone else this question, ask yourself if you truly care, and why you should. If you ask the question and you are not even interested, it's going to show. But there could be any number of reasons why you are in fact interested in the response to the question. Perhaps there was a speaker comment you missed or wanted to make sure you understood. Maybe you are in the midst of planning a speaker-led event yourself. Once you are clear on why you care, then you can form the most fruitful follow-up questions.

What's your take on the new CEO at (fill in the blank)?

A variation of this question might be, "What's your take on the first-round draft picks?" Asking about the latest corporate- or sports-news event of the moment can lead to a conversation about all kinds of things—employment histories and favorite sports teams are just the beginning. The corporate twist, especially, often leads to the "What do you do?" question.

What's your view of the recent foreign policy changes?

Opening a political discussion with someone you've just met might be stepping into a minefield, but it can be a great way to probe your connection with someone who is already an acquaintance. This type of question, of course, alludes to political dispositions without flat-out asking about them. It can also lead to any number of other topics. If you weave in a reference to where you read a particular tidbit, for instance, that can open up a discussion about the state of the media today. Querying people about their political opinions can lead to extremely engaging and emotionally charged conversations. Politics tend to reveal the ways people are either united or polarized. If both of you are enjoying the back and forth, keep going. If things get too heated, sidestep conflict with a more conciliatory remark such as, "I'll have to give that perspective some thought."

Pose a Hypothetical

A variation on asking for someone's opinion is to ask what the person thinks of a hypothetical situation. These queries are thought-provoking and often coax people out of their pat-response patterns. Hypothetical questions are best used after a bit of small talk, once a connection has been formed but is still growing in strength. These questions can reveal unexpected things about people to one another, and can range from the professional to the personal, from the practical to the fanciful: "How would you handle it if you received a promotion over one of your closest colleagues?" "What decision would you have made about that situation if you were CEO?" "What would be the first three things you'd do if you won the lottery?"

When posing hypothetical questions, you want to stay sensitive to the fact that these types of questions can deepen the conversation, but if used in the wrong way they may seem invasive or off-putting. You can diffuse the potential for discomfort by prefacing the question with preliminary queries such as, "Do you mind if I pick your brain about something?" or "I'm dealing with a thorny problem—can I pose a hypothetical situation to you and get your opinion?"

Some people do especially well with these types of questions. Think back to the communication-style matrix in Chapter 3. Zig Zags and Circles love hypothetical questions, the Zig Zags for their intellectual framework and idea-exploring premises, the Circles for the personal aspects of the questions and how they might be able to help puzzle out solutions. When choosing whether to use a hypothetical question as a conversation starter, you may want to determine the person's communication style first to see if the individual may be open to this level of inquiry.

Seek Advice

Advice is a powerful conversation opener in cases when the other person can actually be of assistance. When people can provide assistance, it makes them feel helpful. This creates a positive mood memory, a concept that's covered in detail in Chapter 8. Be clear about the questions you ask, however broad or specific they may be, so that they accurately reflect your interest. If you ask something that, as it turns out, the other person can't help with, then follow up by asking if the person has any ideas about how you can find the information you're after. Being able to give even general advice makes most people feel good and more prone to connecting to you.

Can you tell me how to get to . . . ?

This opener can be a little tricky because the person responding will probably expect that once you get the directions you need (e.g., to the bar, the hotel spa, etc.), that will be the end of the conversation. Still, it can be a natural and straightforward way to approach someone. If someone asks you this type of question, offer to escort them and chat along the way.

Which do you suggest?

Depending on the environment you're in, you might ask for a recommendation about a breakout session, a course, a restaurant, or a hotel—you fill in the blank. This type of question is an easy conversation starter and allows for a simple follow-up: "How come?" You could also ask something more specific based on the other person's response, such as, "Is the content of the session basic or advanced?" or "What dish do you recommend?" "Is the professor a tough grader?"

Compliment

To compliment someone is to express praise, commendation, or admiration. A compliment is the exact opposite of flattery, because by definition flattery is fake or insincere. Compliments are signs of respect. Of course, you must be genuine in your compliment, lest it come off as flattery, but if there is something that you truly admire and want to express about someone, giving the person a compliment can be a great way to open a conversation. Not only does it create positive energy between you and the person you're addressing, it can also build trust and foster greater understanding. When people realize that you've noticed something positive about them, chances are they'll start looking for things they admire about you, too. This technique is often most effective when followed by a supporting question that reflects your genuine feelings and curiosity.

I love that shirt/tie/scarf/jacket/necklace.
One obvious but helpful follow-up to this kind of compliment is, "Where did you get it?" I once admired a necklace a woman was wearing and when I asked where she'd found it, she replied, "Ireland." Her response led us into an energizing conversation about travel, one of my favorite vices. The "where" follow-up can get you talking about any number of topics: shopping, traditions, or family keepsakes, for instance. You'll never know until you ask.

I thought the question you asked was really interesting.
In my experience, this comment is suitable when in the audience at a conference, speaker, or roundtable event. You can then follow up this compliment with a question: "What did you think of the person's response?" Another version of this technique works well when building connections with your coworkers. If someone has handled a business situation in an admirable way, compliment your colleague on it, then ask the person how and why he chose to handle it in that manner. Not only will you learn more about people through their responses—and possibly improve your own professional interpersonal skills—but you'll also strike the right mood memory with the people you're addressing, making them feel helpful and recognized.

Use the News: The Events-Based Inquiry

This type of inquiry can be related to the event you're attending, a current event from the morning paper, or even a simple life event such as buying a car. Use the event as a reference point to generate conversation about broad opinions and specific details, and use responses to continue enriching the conversation. Here are some examples, with suggestions for following up on possible responses.

Have you been to this event before?
Use the response to discuss similar events, asking follow-up questions about how this event compares to others the person may have attended or upcoming events that may be of interest.

What do you think about that (fill in the blank) news story?
Choosing a widely covered current event will open up more possible paths of conversation than asking about something obscure. Follow-up questions could range from the plight of the people involved in the story, to the ways in which different media outlets are covering it, to previous events that current circumstances call to mind. If someone hasn't heard of or been following the news, that person won't have much to say about it, of course. You can handle this situation by quickly sketching in the story for the other person or simply introducing a new topic of conversation.

Have you ever owned a Honda?
Asking ordinary, everyday questions such as this one can be surprisingly revealing. Someone you've just met or are still getting to know is likely to feel comfortable giving opinions about something as neutral as a consumer product, and this type of question makes most people feel that you value their opinion enough to ask it. Follow-up questions can lead to conversations about the price of gas, the manufacturing methods of different countries, even road trip memories—you name it.

LIVE THE LAW: *CREATE MORE OPTIONS*

So far I have provided you with a few examples of each type of conversation opener. Now it's time to expand your conversation comfort level and come up with your own. Here is your challenge:

For each type of conversation starter discussed—personal, opinion, hypothetical, advice questions, compliments, and event-based inquiries—look over the examples and change them in some way to make them authentic for you. Then generate at least two more original examples for each type. At the end of the exercise you should have a robust repertoire of questions to use for opening and continuing conversations in any situation.

The Art of Probing

To sustain an engaged conversation, you've got to learn the art of the probe. A probe is a question that digs deeper into the topic being discussed, opening up new material to explore. You've already read some examples of probing questions in the previous sections. Probes are excellent conversation continuers once the initial spark of dialogue has been lit.

Even the most curious people, full of probing questions, sometimes find themselves in conversations where they suddenly hit a brick wall. When that happens it is helpful to follow the lead of the person you're talking to. What has most excited this person during the conversation so far? If you hit a topic and the other person's energy flags, move on to a new topic until you land on one that helps the dialogue flow again. The more energetic responses you get, the better your chances for continuing to probe in ways that build connection.

There are three main types of probes: clarifying, rational, and expansion.

Clarifying Probe: Am I Clear?

A *clarifying probe* effectively demonstrates that you are paying attention. Rephrase or summarize what you've heard and ask if you've understood it correctly, or, if you don't think you have understood, ask the other person to explain in greater detail. Clarifying probes are also great conversation stallers because, if you are thinking about where you want to take the conversation next, they'll buy you time. Be careful about how you phrase these kinds of probes, though. Avoid constructions such as "Are you saying . . . ?" which, depending on tone and whom you're talking to, can be misperceived as shock, judgment, or even outrage. Instead, paraphrase what you think you heard and then check your accuracy with, "Did I understand that correctly?"

Rational Probe: How Come?

A *rational probe* seeks to understand the reasoning behind a stated choice or action. Another way to think about this probe is that it asks "How come?" instead of "Why?"

Intentionally or not, *why* is a word that almost instantly puts the receiver on the defensive. It makes people feel as if they are being challenged and must defend their responses. "How come?" poses more of a genuine inquiry, lessening the possibility that the question will be construed as some kind of attack. To minimize this possibility further, watch your tone of voice and rate of speech. Longer phrasing such as "I'm curious, what made you opt for that project over the other one?" feels more thought out and less aggressive than a super-fast "How come?"

Resist the common urge, though, to express comprehension by filling in the blank with your own response; for example, saying, "How come? Is it because of such-and-such?" instead of just simply "How come?" Providing possible answers to your own question before the other person has time to respond shuts down the flow of communication and could make the other person feel as if you don't really want to hear what she has to say.

Expansion Probe: Elaborate Please?

An *expansion probe* delves for more information about a given response. My favorite phrase is, "Tell me more." This statement invites people to elaborate on something that interests them, which naturally makes them feel comfortable. It also lets them know that you are genuinely interested in hearing what they're talking about, putting them at ease that they are not dominating the conversation. Expansion probes allow you to listen (there's more about listening in Chapter 6) and learn what the other person's authentic interests, needs, and concerns are—and how you might be able to help. These opportunities to assist rise up organically in conversations and can be powerful opportunities for further growing connections. Remember, it's not about you, it's about the relationship.

Don't Interrogate

As already discussed, with any of these questioning techniques, don't ask unless you want to know the answer. If you don't really care, you are more likely to tune out when the other person responds. Silence descends, and there is no place else to take the conversation.

When you ask about something of true interest, though, your follow-up questions come to you more easily and your body language and energy naturally reflect your interest and attentiveness. But be careful not to let your exuberance tip over into a machine-gun questioning style. Bombarding people with rapid queries, regardless of your enthusiasm, will make them feel as if they need to protect themselves, and they'll stay guarded.

Enjoy the conversation; don't turn it into an interrogation. Conversations are two-sided dialogues, filled with pauses and spontaneous asides during which the people conversing consider and absorb what is being said by others. Sprinkling in information about yourself is important, because it helps build the bond that good communication promotes, making you more likable and making whomever you're talking to feel comfortable enough to share.

Stay Curious

If we remain curious, then in conversations we appear comfortable and genuine, even without too much foreknowledge of the person we're speaking with. Curiosity brings out the best in us and prompts us to naturally do all those things that foster positive connections: maintain good eye contact, give appropriate head nods, ask interesting follow-up questions that show we're engaged. When we demonstrate these behaviors it's because curiosity does away with distractions and uncertainties. We're focused on connecting, and so that's naturally what we do.

TO GOOGLE OR NOT TO GOOGLE

The twenty-first century has put a new twist on the age-old networking question: Should you do research before attending an event? With the Internet at our 24/7 disposal, we can now spend hours researching people, venues, and events, past, present, and future.

Some experts may counsel you to search every bit of information you can before meeting a person or attending an event. I understand the position. And it can certainly increase the range of topics you'll have to be curious about. But my question is, How genuinely curious can you be if you already know all the answers? And if you know so much about a person in advance, won't the actual encounter feel awkward and forced, and won't the other person sense that?

The premise of this entire book is that if our approach to connecting with other people is too calculated, it comes off as fake and is far less effective than if we are genuine in our intent. You may even become uncomfortable knowing too much about a person in advance, and that person may sense some weirdness in you. I do think there is some middle ground on this question. I firmly believe in doing some solid research about a company or industry before attending an interview or targeted event. You don't want to be a know-it-all, but you do want to be well-informed. But obsessively Googling people and getting clogged with information about them before you've even established a genuine connection can block all the natural pathways to creating a bond.

When I was meeting with a rather well-known CEO, I did a Wikipedia search on him and spent all of five minutes reading the entry before turning to something else. The quick research hit broadened my knowledge of his career, which was helpful, but I didn't learn so much about him that I had nothing to learn about him during our lunch appointment. Somehow I did end up telling him that he had a Wikipedia entry, and he was so enthralled that he pulled out his BlackBerry to check it out right then and there. We shared a laugh. But the key was that I didn't overdo the research.

There is no perfect answer to this quandary, so you must decide what feels right for you. My advice: Do enough research that you have a solid base of background knowledge, but don't go overboard. There should still be plenty you want to know because, after all, this is the essence of curiosity. When prepping for a meeting or an event, do your due diligence but don't get sucked completely into the maw of the Internet. Be curious, but don't be a stalker.

Refresh Your Memory

The Law of Curiosity. Curiosity creates connections.

Start by Being Curious. Harness your curiosity to initiate conversations and open up avenues of dialogue.

Learn How to Ask Questions. Open-ended questions create opportunities for conversation; probing questions are the follow-ups that deepen the connection the conversation creates.

Don't Interrogate. Stay curious, and continue asking questions to help the conversation unfold in fruitful new directions, but remember that a discussion is a two-sided thing. Sharing yourself is part of the experience, and a key part of building the connection.

Restrain Your Internet Tendencies. Use the Internet to prep for events and meetings and build background knowledge, but don't go overboard. Knowing too much puts you in a position where there's nothing left to know, deadening curiosity and taking away that path to true communication. Moderate yourself.

6

The Law of Listening

"A good listener is not only popular everywhere, but after a while he knows something."

—Wilson Mizner, playwright

One of my executive coaching clients, Jed, is a partner at a leading ad agency. While discussing the impact of good listening, he related a story to me about two young hires, Gerri and Ethan, with whom he'd been working. Gerri and Ethan were both fresh out of college when they joined the agency, with no previous advertising experience. As their team leader, Jed asked them each to sketch out campaign ideas to present to him directly after client meetings so that he could critique their work and help train them as efficiently as possible.

During one initial meeting with a beverage-company client, the client kept using the word *fresh* when describing the ad campaign he wanted. In the campaign proposals to Jed afterward, Gerri, who's athletic and an avid hiker, envisioned presenting the product using an outdoor scene of a family enjoying nature. Ethan, who was in a rock band in college, heard "fresh" and thought the client wanted something hip, with lots of young people in the scene.

"Those ideas aren't fresh!" Jed said to them when he saw their proposed campaigns. "I've seen both these types of commercials loads of times. When the client says he wants something 'fresh,' he means he wants something he's never seen before. When you're meeting with clients, you have to listen to everything they're saying. You can't just hear what you think they're saying—that's how you get yourselves in trouble."

The next time the team met with the client about the beverage product, Jed was impressed with how attentive Gerri and Ethan were. Each appeared alert and interested, and asked good questions at appropriate moments. Afterward they collaborated on their follow-up presentation to Jed and suggested an innovative campaign involving animation. Jed liked it so much that he shared it with the rest of the team, and the concept wound up being the inspiration for the campaign the team eventually designed—and which the client loved.

Just as curiosity is all about asking focused, engaged questions to find connections, listening is all about actively hearing and absorbing what is being said. Listening is not a passive activity. It takes energy and concentration to focus on what people are saying and what they mean by it, and to not just hear what you *think* they mean by it or what you *want* them to mean by it.

Regardless of where you are in your career, listening is a skill that you must continue to work on. Even executives and colleagues in upper management can find that, while they may listen to what their junior colleagues say, they may not do it as effectively as they could. Listening is a skill that takes constant vigilance. How you listen is just as vital to strong communication as what you say, and it has just as much impact on your likability. It is crucial to do it effectively.

Listen to Understand

As humans, we fundamentally want and need to be understood, and this applies in all realms of our lives, from the personal to the professional. But being understood requires receptive listening on the other end. If we want others to understand us, we need to learn how to truly listen to and understand them. When building relationships, how you listen can be as important as what you have to say. This is the foundation of the *law of listening*: You have to listen to understand.

Too often we get caught up in our own agendas, concerns, and intentions, and listen on only a surface level. Effective listening is the single most powerful thing you can do to build and maintain a climate of trust and collaboration. Strong listening skills are the foundation for all solid relationships. By listening we can:

- Build trust
- Assess needs
- Identify interests and passions
- Discover commonalities
- Tune in to emotions and energy
- Determine communication preferences
- Uncover known or unidentified concerns

And in the workplace, good listening is also what enables you to:

- Determine what motivates an employee
- Sell more effectively
- Understand the root causes of issues or miscommunications
- Reduce conflict
- Collaborate and innovate with others

Comprehending what you hear, and acting on that comprehension, is fundamental to cultivating connections that allow for personal and professional growth.

Know What Level You Are Listening On

Before we can harness our listening skills to the optimum effect, we need to understand where we are listening from. Think of this as listening at different levels, all of which serve different intentions in the conversation and are collectively important in building relationships. In a way, the different levels reflect the varying degrees of focus and effort required in different settings. As you become more aware of how and when you are listening, you will be able to move more fluidly between the levels as the conversation or situation warrants.

Level 1: Listening In

Inward listening is the most basic level of listening. It is the process of taking what is being said and finding a way to relate it to yourself, filtering what you hear through your own experience. An example puts it in simple terms: When a friend says, "I love that color blue," and you answer either, "Oh, me too!" or "No, I prefer darker shades." You are responding based on your own preferences and opinions, whether consciously or unconsciously.

Most people listen on this level most of the time because it is easy and comfortable. It can also be effective. "Listening in" is extremely valuable for establishing commonalities, a component that is critical to creating connections and increasing likability. When we listen on this level, we take in what is being said from our own perspective, finding the ways we can relate to it, which contributes to the development of the conversation. Sharing your views, thoughts, or experiences helps you express empathy. This level of listening fosters self-disclosure, which can make other people feel trusted, which in turn can make them feel more comfortable opening up. By opening up in this way and conveying how you think or feel about the subject at hand, you also communicate your willingness to participate in a dialogue, which also builds trust.

Of course, when taken too far and overrelied on, this level of listening can be limiting. Remember, this is about *listening*, not seizing the chance to make it all about you. Once I was at a conference talking amicably with a group of other professionals. Another woman came up to the group, listened in for a few moments, and then, when someone in this circle mentioned that he had just led a team analyzing the possible applications of new technology within the company, the woman who had just joined the group said, "Me, too!" and she launched into a blow-by-blow account that completely dominated the conversation. No one else could get a word in edgewise. Then I noticed the looks on the other people's faces, which made clear everyone was thinking the same thing: "Can you believe how she's going on?" and "When will she shut up?" Even if we'd wanted to engage this woman, she wasn't giving us the chance to. She clearly wasn't picking up on the nonverbal messages of the group; she wasn't "listening" to what the others were "saying" while she was talking. The situation reminded me of how important it is to not just listen with your ears, but with your eyes, by picking up the unspoken signals others send.

I've introduced inward listening first because it is the most common and easiest place to start, but it is best to combine this level of listening with other techniques, moving back and forth between them as the conversation warrants. Use inward listening to establish trust and confidence and to help the conversation along by opening up. Once groundwork has been established and your initial connection with the other person begins building into a relationship, inward listening helps to further strengthen the bond.

Level 2: Listening Out

With *outward listening*, you are focusing on other speakers and relating what they're saying to what you know about *them*. When you are engaged in this level of listening and your friend says she likes the color blue, your response is more along the lines of, "Blue looks really good on you," or "Why do you like it?" Outward listening leverages the law of curiosity; it's when you use expansion probes and phrases such as "Tell me more about that," and "How come?"

The woman at the conference who commandeered the conversation would have been far more effective if she'd expressed her parallel experience with the man who'd just spoken by using an enthusiastic level-one "Me, too!" and then followed up with a level-two question: "What were the details of your project?" She would have established commonality while at the same time seeking to broaden the conversation, a one-two punch of excellent communication and information exchange. Combining the different levels of listening, and moving back and forth between them when appropriate, is a powerful way to build connections through listening.

Level 3: Listening Intuitively

Intuitive listening expands on level-two listening, but instead of just focusing on what the person is saying with his voice, you are paying attention to how it is being said, and to what is not being said. You are picking up on the speaker's body language and the general vibe you get from the speaker, as well as the words. Intuitive listening is about hearing more than the words that are spoken. When we listen intuitively, we are attuned to the speaker's tone, facial expressions, and stance. When you are engaged in intuitive listening, you notice that when your friend says she likes the color blue, she does so with a tranquil note in her voice, and you respond, "You seem so calm when you say that. Do you find that color soothing?" You pick up on what is being said, verbalize your perception, and ask for confirmation of it.

To date, my most powerful experience with intuitive listening occurred when I was taking my coaching certification course. Part of the training was to do coaching sessions with other students in groups of three. I was working with my fellow students Ellie and Naomi. It was Naomi's turn to be the client and Ellie's turn to be the coach, and I was in the role of observer. Naomi had just gotten married, and she chose the subject of when to have kids as the topic of her coaching session. She launched into a rational analysis, pointing out that her husband was still in business school, and that she was just starting to build her own business. On the other hand, she countered, she was past thirty and worried about waiting too long. Ellie intermittently intervened with questions to advance Naomi's exploration of the idea.

Suddenly Ellie said to Naomi, "I get the sense that you're ready to have kids but don't want to admit it, because you're afraid your husband isn't ready. Is that possible?" Naomi stared at her like a deer caught in headlights. Ellie had been listening to what Naomi said, but knowing her classmate a little by this point, she also listened to *how* she said it. "I think you're right," Naomi said, "I am ready. I couldn't figure out why I was unsettled about it until you said that just now." By comprehending both the verbal and non-verbal clues, Ellie helped Naomi articulate what she truly felt and thought. Naomi broached the subject with her husband, even though she was hesitant to do so, and it turned out he felt he was ready, too. Two months later she was pregnant.

The key with intuitive listening is to not assume your interpretation of what the person is "saying" is correct. Ellie handled that perfectly, for two reasons: One, she expressed her own interpretation of the situation by using the phrase, "I get the sense . . . ," and two, she followed up her statement by asking for confirmation, adding, "Is that possible?" She didn't try to flat-out tell Naomi what she was saying/thinking, as if it was a foregone conclusion, and she checked the accuracy of her assertion by asking Naomi what she thought.

Intuitive listening does not just happen in personal situations. It is extremely effective—critical, even—in professional settings as well. It helps you home in on the nuances of communication and hear the unspoken message. When my coaching client Aaron was promoted, one of his new direct reports was a colleague named Shawn, who'd been his peer before the promotion. Soon after this seniority change was announced, Aaron noticed that Shawn's behavior toward him seemed to shift. Shawn began responding to Aaron's questions in a curt fashion, rarely making eye contact and fidgeting restlessly whenever Aaron spoke during meetings.

Aaron spoke to me about his belief that the change in Shawn's behavior had to do with the fact he had been promoted and Shawn had not. He acknowledged that he wasn't sure if this was the correct assessment of the situation, so we set out a plan of action to find out. Aaron asked Shawn if they could get together, and he opened their meeting by saying, "I want to address any concerns or discomfort that may exist about the recent change in our roles. Can you help me understand how we might best move forward?"

Shawn was reluctant to discuss the situation at first. Aaron continued to probe by asking, "How can I help you continue to grow professionally?" Once Shawn believed that Aaron truly wanted to create a positive work environment, the conversation began to turn. Shawn opened up about how he felt he'd stopped being given new opportunities at work. As a result of the conversation, Aaron was able to make sure Shawn was put on projects that would let him continue developing his skill sets, and Shawn became one of the most effective employees on Aaron's new team. By listening intuitively to Shawn and engaging him in conversation, Aaron was able to take an uncomfortable and possibly unproductive dynamic and turn it into something that was mutually beneficial.

Intuitive listening makes people feel as if the other person relates to, empathizes with, and validates them. On a very deep level, it makes them feel *heard*, so the ability to listen intuitively is a very likable trait. It builds confidence in the connection and helps the speaker feel as if his needs are being understood and addressed.

The key to effective intuitive listening is to know when it is appropriate. It is impossible to maintain this level of engagement all the time; it's simply too exhausting. And if you demonstrate intuitive listening with people you've only recently met or don't know well, it could seem off-putting to them to be "read" in this way. Use your judgment, and remember that alternating between the three levels of listening at the appropriate moments is the best way to harness the natural give-and-take of a conversation.

When you do engage in intuitive listening, be thoughtful with your tone of voice to make it clear that you are proposing and not assuming, and stay open to being wrong. It is not a bad thing to be wrong in your intuitive listening; it can actually open the door for further connection. Getting to the essence of something is a process, and that is what communication is all about.

Listen Up!

A key part of successful communication, then, is recognizing *what* level of listening you are engaged in. Now you must build your skills by learning *how* to listen more effectively.

Get Off Your Pedestal

In the opening story of this chapter, Gerri and Ethan at first can reference only their own definitions of the word *fresh*. Well, the Merriam-Webster dictionary lists more than fifteen different ways "fresh" can be used. Gerri and Ethan's problem was that they were consulting only the abridged versions of their own dictionaries, defaulting to the first definition that sprang to mind for each of them.

It only makes sense that we all process information differently, compiling it into our individual dictionaries. How we respond to situations is shaped by what we have already experienced, and these experiences are our reference points.

Put another way, this is what I like to call your pedestal. We spend our lives piling up information, experiences, and encounters, and when we're in new situations we view them from atop these stockpiles of personal knowledge that we have accumulated over the years. These piles are our pedestals. Although pedestal building is natural, the problem is that no one else is up there with us; no one looks out at the world with the exact same viewpoint we do.

That's why it is so critical to stay open to the notion that our perceptions might not be entirely accurate, and to continually ask ourselves, "How else can I interpret this situation?" By staying mindful of different possibilities and realities, we create opportunities for increased communication, understanding, and connection.

Use your clarifying probes to further your comprehension of other people's perspectives, then employ intuitive listening to grasp their full meanings. Step into someone else's shoes to appreciate their way of thinking—in other words, *get off your pedestal*!

Listen with Your Eyes

We've just learned how intuitive listening is about listening to what's being communicated nonverbally as much as verbally. It's about listening with your eyes as well as with your ears. The woman at the conference who suddenly hijacked an otherwise amiable group conversation was oblivious to this concept. Had she been listening with her eyes, she would have "heard" that the others in the group may have had things to contribute but felt as if they were shut out of the conversation while she was talking. As a result, she closed herself off to deepening her connections with that group of associates.

We are constantly in situations where it's valuable to listen with our eyes. When discussing a possible new project with a group of direct reports, the ones who perk up at the description of the assignment are the ones who we sense have the most enthusiasm, even if they haven't said so explicitly. Hearing it with our eyes may result in assigning them to the project. When we notice that a boss has forgotten a junior colleague's name, we might slip the information naturally into the conversation to help the boss out.

This technique can be extremely helpful when determining the right moment to close a conversation, too. Is your client looking at her watch and starting to gather her papers? Take the cue that it's time to wrap things up. If you are unsure, provide an out for the other person by remarking, "I don't want to take too much of your time," or "Would you like some time to think about it?" If the person doesn't take the bait, you know that she still wants to stay engaged in the current conversation. Use your eyes to hear what's being expressed in nonverbal ways.

Catch Your Drift: Dealing with Distractions

Active listening can be difficult, in part because the mind is so easily distracted. Passively nodding is one thing, but to really listen you must be alert and attuned. You must be focused.

To make things even more difficult, distractions can compound the distractions. I can't count how many times I've been in the middle of a conversation and suddenly remembered something unrelated that I'd been trying to remember. At that point, I am distracted not just by the thought, but by the process of trying to remember the thought. The result, of course, is that it becomes extremely challenging to give someone my undivided attention.

Over the years I've learned some techniques that help me manage my internal interruptions and stop my mind from drifting.

Just Say It

When my mind is caught up in a distraction, the best way for me to handle it isn't to cover it up but rather to simply say something about it. I don't blurt out, "Hold on, I'm distracted, I have to cancel my dentist appointment." But I do find a way to take a mental pause while letting the speaker know I'm still interested in what they are saying. In these circumstances I'll just say, "Give me a moment. I don't want to miss the rest of this story, but I've just remembered something I don't want to forget."

By putting words to your passing thoughts, you lessen the chance that you'll nonverbally signal, through your facial expressions and body language, that you are distracted and disinterested in the other person. Instead, you can reaffirm that you are interested in what is being said, because you are taking a quick second to eliminate the distraction so that you can prioritize the conversation at hand. Make a habit of this technique. Employ other methods as well (as detailed in the next sections), but always use them in conjunction with the "just say it" rule.

Jot It Down

One of the most effective ways to eliminate distractions is to write them down. Try to carry a pen and paper on you at all times, and at those moments when you can't, use the note-taking or voice-recording application on your smartphone.

This can also be an extremely effective method for preventing future distractions. When you are in the middle of a meeting or a conversation and hear something or have a thought that you don't want to forget, write it down. It will prevent you from getting distracted trying to remember it later. You don't need to copy things down in full sentences; just capture a few key words or phrases to jolt your memory and help bring the thoughts back to the surface when you look at the notes later on.

Invite Them Along

I was at a neighborhood party one evening soon after we'd moved to a new town, and didn't know anyone there except my husband. Famished, I only half-jokingly said to my new neighbors that I was so distracted by my hunger I couldn't follow the conversation until the guy with the chicken skewers came back around. Attempting to lure the hors d'oeuvres bearers to our corner of the room became a game. It turned out that I wasn't the only one who hadn't had a chance to eat before the event, and our joking around was a great icebreaker that kept the conversation flowing for the rest of the night.

Thirst is another distraction that can have a positive spin. When excusing yourself to the bar, ask if you can bring drinks back for the people you've been speaking with. This shows your consideration as well as your interest in continuing the conversation. Or you can ask if anyone wants to join you in heading to the bar. It's another great way to stay in conversation with one or two people from the group and possibly mingle with new people at the same time as you proceed through the crowd.

Interject, or Postpone and Follow Up

Sometimes our minds drift because we're tired and not all that interested in the topic of conversation at hand. When that happens, try to rejuvenate the discussion. An interesting new topic can inject unexpected energy into the situation. Use a question or story about something related to the current conversation to lead it down a new path. Don't abruptly go off-topic, because that will feel jarring to most other people, but try to tap into the stimulation that a lively discussion holds.

For those times when you are simply too exhausted to muster the energy it takes to connect, it's best to just be honest about it and see if you can postpone the discussion. We're all busy, and people truly do understand exhaustion. Go ahead and "just say it," and find out if you can reschedule. The key here is ensuring that the other person doesn't feel blown off. You want to communicate that the encounter is important to you, but you are currently not in the best state to engage or connect. Demonstrate your willingness to reengage later by following up, and following up fast. Since you were the one to postpone, take the initiative to make the next meeting happen.

How Well Do You Listen?

During my first week in business school, one of my professors said, "Society is an easier place for the extrovert." This is a provocative statement, and I've continued thinking about it over the years. I do agree that it's basically true, but I also think introverts possess unique skills that are extremely helpful when building relationships and growing connections. Introverts tend to think before they speak and listen before they talk. They are more inclined to ask than to tell, and this makes them far better suited than extroverts to embrace the laws of curiosity and listening.

Being aware of your listening style, understanding how natural listening is for you and where you might improve your skills, is one of the first steps in harnessing the full power of the law of listening. Listening is a crucial skill, and it is one that can be acquired. So work on making your skills even better.

LIVE THE LAW: *HOW IS YOUR LISTENING?*

We all have natural strengths as listeners, and we all have ways in which we can improve our listening skills. Review the list of listening traits in Table 6-1. In one column are those traits that denote good listening; in the other are common behaviors that get in the way of listening effectively. Put check marks next to the three traits in the DO list that you want to actively work on to enhance your listening skills. Then circle the items you are already doing well, to reinforce those good listening habits. In the DON'T column, check the three traits you are most prone to and that you want to tone down.

Table 6-1. Listening traits.

DO	DON'T
Maintain eye contact	Interrupt
Limit your talking	Show signs of impatience
Focus on the speaker	Judge or argue mentally
Ask questions	Multitask during a conversation
Manage your emotions	Project your ideas
Listen with your eyes and ears	Think about what to say next
Listen for ideas and opportunities	Have expectations or preconceived ideas
Remain open to the conversation	Become defensive or assume you are being attacked
Confirm understanding, paraphrase	Use condescending, aggressive, or closed body language
Give nonverbal messages that you are listening (nod, smile)	Listen with biases or closed to new ideas
Ignore distractions	Jump to conclusions or finish someone's sentences

Improve Your Listening

Remember, we all have room for improvement. First, give yourself credit for the things you are already doing well. Consciously acknowledging our strengths reinforces them.

Next, review the behaviors that you've determined you need to work on, and make a plan. How are you going to improve your listening in this area? Reread the Catch Your Drift section for some ideas on managing mental interruptions and maintaining your mental focus. Everyone's plan will be different.

You can also convert your weaknesses into strengths by using them as connection points in conversation. If you know that "limit your talking" is something you want to work on (because during conversations you are prone to enthusiastically interjecting in a way that can come off as interrupting), tell people in a light but forthright tone, "If I interrupt, just stop me." For people who already do a good job of appropriately limiting their talking, it can be jarring to feel as if they've been interrupted. By asking them to flag the "interrupting" behavior when you do it, you accomplish two things: You make the other person aware that you are actively trying to be a better listener, and you get help noticing when the negative behavior kicks in. The more that you notice this behavior, the easier it will be to correct it. If at first you need help realizing when you're doing it, don't feel bad. Soon you'll start catching it yourself and be able to adjust it on your own.

Good Listening Is a Win-Win

Listening on deeper levels is not just about paying close attention to the other person. It is about actively participating in building the relationship. And it is also about you. As an effective listener, you will establish stronger connections with the people you engage, you'll have a more robust understanding of what is being said, and you'll get more out of conversations on the whole.

Natan, a former client of mine and now a friend, verbalized this idea so well to me one day. I had expressed how much I enjoyed talking to him, in part because I felt like he really listened to me. "You make me feel as if you are hanging on my every word," I remember saying. "I feel not only listened to, but cared about." Natan smiled and said, "I wasn't always such a great listener." It wasn't until he realized how *not* listening well made people feel disconnected and ignored that he slowed down and began trying to really listen. And when he did, he explained, "I saw how much I'd been missing from most conversations!" He considered his efforts to enhance his listening skills the single most beneficial thing he'd done yet to improve his life, both personally and professionally.

Listening well is a pathway to implementing other laws of likability. In the previous chapter we've seen how it serves the law of curiosity. In Chapter 7, we'll discuss how it can enhance the law of similarity, and in Chapter 8 we'll look at how it impacts what I call "mood memory." Listening is a powerful building block: Continue improving your listening skills and your likability will naturally increase.

Refresh Your Memory

The Law of Listening. You have to listen to understand.

Listen to Understand. If we want others to understand us, we have to understand them by truly listening to what they are communicating.

Harness the Three Levels of Listening. Inward listening (level one) relates what you hear to *you*, and it helps establish commonalities and conversational ease. Outward listening (level two) relates what you hear to the speaker; it leverages the law of curiosity to uncover interests and perspectives. Listening intuitively (level three) is a powerful way to gain a deeper understanding of the situation and possibly even help the speaker put words to things she hasn't as yet been expressing verbally.

How You Listen Is Key. To encourage communication and build meaningful connections, get off your pedestal and listen from other people's perspectives. And don't forget, sometimes good listening is done with your eyes as well as your ears.

Manage Distractions. Articulate when you need to regain your focus (just say it!), jot down thoughts so that you won't be distracted trying to remember them later, and if you are too exhausted to muster the energy to truly engage, postpone and reschedule.

Improve Your Listening. Take credit for the ways you already listen well, and note the areas where you can improve. Then set up a plan to work on those things.

Good Listening Is a Win-Win. Not only does listening well make people feel heard and understood, it also enhances your experience of the situation and of the connection.

7

The Law of Similarity

"Much of the vitality in a friendship lies in the honoring of differences, not simply in the enjoyment of similarities."

—James L. Fredericks, theologian

Early in my career I worked for a bank and was assigned a new project with a vendor whose CEO was a man named Mateo. By all outward appearances, Mateo and I were different on every front: gender, age, religion, ethnicity, education, hobbies, career level, family lives. He was a thirty-something techie who was married with three children. He spoke his native Ukrainian with his family and adhered closely to his culture's traditions. I was a single twenty-something MBA whose only responsibilities and priorities were work and fun.

The project required ongoing communication and collaboration to ensure that the customization of the technology we were working on met the business needs we were developing it for. I must admit that I didn't think Mateo and I would be a good fit. In my mind, working with this man did not sound fun. But it was. Once we dove into the project, we completely and unexpectedly clicked. We found that we had very similar work approaches. We both enjoyed thinking outside the box and relished tackling whatever new challenge was at hand. We shared a quick, tongue-in-cheek sense of humor and an enthusiasm for creative problem solving.

Despite not having obvious things in common, we had many similarities when it came to professional attitudes and management styles, and we worked extremely well together—so well, in fact, that Mateo eventually recruited me away from the company that was employing me to work directly for him. He became one of my most valued mentors, and also a treasured friend. He was supportive of my leaving the finance world and starting my own business, and shared great wisdom when I followed in his married-with-children path. Our similar attitudes and styles were points of true connection that continued deepening as we worked together. We both appreciated these similarities, perhaps even more so because we were so dissimilar in so many ways. The connection we formed enriched our professional and eventually our personal lives.

In movies and TV shows, one of the most common ways to denote that a character is a regular in a restaurant or bar is for him to walk in, sit down, and say, "I'll have the usual." Why is that storytelling shorthand so effective, and what makes it so homey and appealing? One reason is that we are comforted by what we know. We relate to this "I'll have the usual" mentality because, on a basic level, we understand why the character goes to the same establishment again and again.

Realizing that we share a connection with someone else puts us at ease, whatever the parallel is. It may be that we know the same people, have a fondness for the same place, or have had similar life experiences. Finding those authentic similarities and associations increases your comfort with new people and, likewise, their comfort with you, and feeling at ease not only makes conversation easier, but also opens the door to discovering further things you have in common, which provides more links for building connections. The commonalities we have with people are not always obvious at first, but understanding how to stay alert to them is part of the work of building connections into meaningful relationships.

As our careers develop, we sometimes stop looking for commonalities with people we know, assuming that we've gathered all the information we need about them. Broadening our approach to our existing relationships—refinding our curiosity about the people we know, staying aware of things we might share besides just the task at hand—is another powerful way to continue deepening connections.

People Like People Like Them

When we meet someone with whom we have strong similarities, our comfort level quickly increases; the conversation flows and the likability is palpable. This is the *law of similarity*: People like people who are like them.

This doesn't mean, of course, that sparks are going to fly whenever you meet someone like you. Sometimes the similarities might be too strong, and you'll come up against the same traits you're not fond of in yourself. At these moments it is important to step back if you can and assess your resistance.

It's also true that sometimes the similarities are explicit and direct, and other times they are more subtle and only come to light over time. When we uncover our similarities, though, we can create opportunities for deeper—and more lasting—authentic connections. The road to likability can become shorter and less winding. As comfort increases, conversation becomes more open, nurturing trust. Likability is not a given, but commonality is a powerful starting point.

It's All About Trust

As we saw in Chapter 3, people look to other people to affirm the impressions they have of people and things. This is how we form our perceptions, and a key part of the process is validating and corroborating our opinions with other trusted sources of information.

We look to other people in our industry to recommend a software solution or a vendor; we schedule an interview with a job candidate because one of our colleagues had a positive experience working with the candidate a few years back. This is the *law of association*, which is the law of similarity's sublaw: People trust the sources they know best.

It's the same principle that applies when you're fixed up on a blind date by someone you know. You think, "Beth knows him, and Beth knows me, so I can trust that at the very least he's a decent, normal guy. Beth wouldn't steer me wrong." It's also why so many companies offer referral bonuses to their employees. If they've already got staff members whom they value and trust, then it makes sense to query—and reward—that pool of resources when seeking more employees.

We follow this sublaw all the time, validating our choices because we connect to them through a trusted third party. We ask friends with similar tastes for movie recommendations; we ask our neighbors for the number of a good plumber; we turn to parents with kids the same age as ours for advice about teachers and doctors. If the person we know likes this other person, we reason, then we'll probably like him or her too.

Uncovering Commonalities

There are so many different ways we can be similar to or associated with another person. Social media sites such as LinkedIn easily illustrate this point. How many degrees of separation are you away from people you don't even know? I decided to do a quick experiment. I have a few hundred connections on LinkedIn, a fairly average number. I arbitrarily typed "Joe" into the site and found out that I was only one person away from 1,554 Joes I didn't yet know. I was one person away from 927 as-yet-unknown-to-me Sues, and even a less common name, Harold, yielded 334 possible connections from whom I was only one person removed.

Commonalities are all around us, even when they are not at first obvious. Knowing the same people is just one way to draw on the law of similarity. We may discover other areas of similarity as well, such as common experiences, shared beliefs and values, physical and demographic similarities, and shared educational backgrounds or work histories; the list goes on. All these are possible avenues to creating the basis for authentic connection.

You Too, Me Too

Often when we first meet someone we go through an almost ritualized round of questions: Where did you go to school? Where did you grow up? Where do you work? Getting responses that match our own can immediately increase our excitement and interest in the new acquaintance. Finding the commonality leads easily to continued conversation and results in a willingness to open up to further the connection: You graduated from college in what year? Oh, wait, did you know so-and-so? This is the "you too, me too" concept. Similarities that may not be visibly obvious can come to the surface quickly with the right types of questions.

A few years back I attended a workshop about communicating your business services through various media channels. We were doing a pitch session, during which most people in the room stood up and delivered a thirty-second sound bite summarizing their services. While listening to a woman named Maya give her pitch about how she wanted to grow her college placement work with high school students, I remember thinking, "Me too! I want to do more work with high school students." At the end of the session I sought her out and found that she'd been looking for me as well, because something in my pitch resonated with her. We both acted on the "you too, me too" moment, and as a result we are still in touch, offering one another professional feedback and frequently collaborating on service offerings.

Avoid feeling as if you are interviewing someone when you're asking them questions by sharing aspects about yourself. Self-disclosure is key if similarities are going to be effectively unearthed. Mention organizations you belong to, places you've visited or lived, your hobbies and interests. Create opportunities for the other person to discover the commonalities, too. By learning about other people's interests and backgrounds and finding common territory, you gain the capacity for creating stronger relationships. The more you know, the more foundation you have to build on.

That Happened to Me, Too

Discovering parallel life experiences with someone can create an instantaneous connection. These experiences can be as simple as learning how to drive, if there is something relatable about them. Did you learn on a stick shift? Did your dad take you to the empty school parking lot on Sundays and let you practice?

Often, though, the more emotional or personal a disclosure, the deeper the bond when it's shared. Not only does a richly textured experience give you a broader set of things to relate to one another about, it also creates trust. You not only get the sense from the other person that "You get me," but that, "You *really* get me."

Significant related experiences are everywhere, but discovering them takes a willingness on your part to share such information about yourself. I was near my home in New Jersey, waiting for a bus into New York City. There was another woman at the bus stop, and we began to chat. We quickly discovered that her daughter and my son were the same age. I asked her where her daughter went to school, and within seconds realized that her daughter was in my son's class. "You're Brenda's mother!" I blurted out, and we both laughed.

At this point the bus arrived, but we wanted to keep talking, so we made our way to the very back of the bus, the only place we could find two seats together. As we settled in, Brenda's mom, Terri, began sharing with me that she had just been laid off and was looking for work. With my background in career counseling, I started asking questions to see how I could help. She revealed that money had been a serious issue for her growing up, and that she never wanted to go back to penny-pinching again. That resonated with me, and she was so open about her background that I felt comfortable sharing too. It turned out that we were both raised in single-parent homes in which money had been tight.

By the end of our conversation we had a play date for the kids recorded in our BlackBerrys, and a coffee date, minus kids, so that we could keep talking about professional opportunities. During our next encounter I learned that Terri was entering the coaching field. Now, whenever we get together we brainstorm joint work ventures to pursue and give one another support. Because Terri was willing to reveal profound life experiences, and because I could relate, both my son and I gained new friends.

Common Cause

From my late teens right up until I had kids in my thirties, I spent almost every weekend volunteering with rescue dogs. I love animals and was lucky enough to work with an organization that had values and a mission in sync with mine: rehabilitating abandoned and abused dogs so that they could be adopted into loving homes.

During those years, if I was dating someone and felt as if I might really like him, I'd ask him to join me and work with the dogs for the day. An afternoon typically entailed walking and playing with the dogs, watching for issues that would inhibit their ability to be house pets, training them on basic commands, managing aggressive behaviors, socializing them with people and other dogs, and, of course, picking up their poop. What was a completely invigorating and fulfilling day for me turned out to be torture for some of my dates, and this was always a deal breaker for me. There was one guy, though, who had never done this kind of work with animals before, who had never even had a pet, yet was enthralled by the experience. At the end of the afternoon he told me that after working with the dogs, he felt as if a door had been opened for him. Well, that guy, Mike, is now my husband.

Common causes can bring people together in ways that are stronger than many other connections. When we are passionate about a cause, a faith, or a strongly held belief, the experience is emotionally charged and powerful. So when two people share those feelings, the connection can be fast and intense. When I saw Mike patiently help a dog overcome a fear of walking in the street, or tirelessly work to ensure that two sibling puppies found a home together, I knew that this shared passion would strengthen our connection.

Sometimes these shared beliefs are obvious because of the context in which you meet—at a house of worship or at a political rally, for instance. At other times you may need to ask questions to find out if you have these things in common. The tools of curiosity and self-disclosure work hand in hand in this case. Here are some questions you can ask to determine if there are possible connections to be made through your passions and beliefs:

- We just moved to the neighborhood. Can you recommend a local temple/church?
- I want to volunteer locally. Do you have any suggestions?
- I am going to/organizing a fund-raiser for (fill in the blank). Would you like to attend/help?

- What do you think about the current governor?
- Are you happy with the president's recent actions?

Politics and religion are two topics about which many people hold passionate beliefs, so they can be interesting territories to explore. Just stay attuned to rising emotions and consider sidestepping or changing the topic if the conversation becomes too heated or extreme.

LIVE THE LAW: *DIG DEEPER*

You are already familiar with how being curious about another person and continuing to ask questions can initiate and deepen a conversation. Now add a layer: Dig deeper into yourself to uncover the multitude of similarities you may have with other people, rather than simply waiting to uncover the similarities they have with you. Recall and recognize all the associations, passion-driven experiences, and beliefs that have helped shape you into the person you are today.

1. Write down every *organization* with which you have ever been associated. Think broadly. Here are some categories to help get you going. Try to write down at least one organization or group for each category.

- Education (high school, college, career training programs, religious schools)

- School clubs or associations (fraternity, debate club, yearbook, student government, alumni associations)

- Camp, outdoor-leadership programs, or student-exchange programs

- Volunteer activities (walkathons, soup kitchens)

- Sports teams (team member, supporter, fantasy league participant, coach)

- Professional associations (job-function affiliations, culture-based industry organizations)

- Organized hobbies and nonprofessional pursuits (book or amateur photography clubs)

- Parent or community associations (PTA, town committees)

- Military (grew up in a military family, did tours of duty)

2. Recall the major *experiences* that have shaped your life. The big, traumatizing ones probably come to mind quickly, but these aren't always easy to discuss or even appropriate to bring up when you are first getting to know someone. Here are some ideas to help you compile a list of transformative experiences you may want to share with others, along with sample questions that could help stoke a conversation.

- Vacations (Where did you go for your honeymoon? Have you ever taken a cruise? What was the last big family trip you took?)

- Activities (Have you ever run a marathon? Gone skydiving? Restored an antique car?)

- Sports (Did you play on a team growing up? Do you play in a league now? Is your kid on a team? How do you teach your child to be a good sport?)

- Family (Are you taking care of ailing parents? Where do your siblings live? How often do you get to visit with them?)

- Career (How long have you had your current job? Have you ever switched careers? If so, how did you figure out what you wanted to do next?)

- Moves (What's the farthest away from your family you've ever moved? Have you ever lived outside the country?)

3. Imagine that you suddenly had a big chunk of money to give away. Where would you donate it? In other words, what is your *cause*? Jot down all your ideas, then circle your top three picks and put a star next to your number-one choice. What is it? Would you donate the money to a religious organization? A political party? A nonprofit dedicated to environmental sustainability? Understanding your top priorities helps you identify like-minded people and connect with them on these issues. Your beliefs and causes don't need to be in the popular majority for connections to happen; often ties are even stronger when formed between people who are passionate about something most other people overlook.

It's Like Looking in a Mirror

Some similarities we can see. It may be an action or a way of speaking, for instance, and often when we are feeling comfortable in a situation we mirror back those things to another person in some way. This is often an unconscious but distinct way people relate when they are engaged in a conversation and feeling connected.

My sister April and I don't look very much alike, but put us in a room together and someone invariably comments on our similar mannerisms and phrases. They've even said our similarities are uncanny. The truth is, I find myself talking and acting more like April when we are in the same room together than when we are apart. I don't consciously aim for this to happen, but it does. I'm mirroring her. When you are speaking with someone you like, your speech patterns and body language often naturally start reflecting the other person's.

Almost every time I work with teenagers, the mirroring phenomenon takes place. When conducting workshops with this age group, I often ask them to pick a partner with whom they get along well. Then I tell them to talk with their partner about something they're passionate about, or share something about themselves that their partner might not know. After ten minutes or so, I go around the room and "freeze" each pair of talkers. The results are amazing: two girls sitting Indian-style across from one another on the floor; two guys talking, both with their hands in their pockets; a guy and a girl both leaning against the wall as they talk, their legs crossed. In the course of their conversations, they've unconsciously matched one another's body positions. Once I even watched two girls who'd only known each other for about a day and a half begin their conversation while standing, then move to sit on the floor in different positions, and eventually adjust their bodies so that they were both unwittingly lying on the floor, facing one another, knees bent behind them, chins in cupped hands.

The first time I worked with Mateo, we were in a conference room, and I had a PowerPoint presentation projecting onto a screen. The presentation very quickly became a conversation, and soon we were both leaning in toward the laptop, looking at the presentation on the small computer screen instead of the big projector screen. We'd unconsciously mirrored one another's seated positions, and referring jointly to the laptop screen echoed the spirit of similarity and collaboration.

Mirroring often happens without thinking, but it can also be used in conscious ways to express understanding or to impart ease to a situation. If someone is telling you something in an excited way, leaning forward in her chair, it helps communicate your interest if you use body language that mirrors hers, so you lean forward, too. Leaning away would convey detachment, the exact opposite of what we're after, but leaning forward creates a similarity that translates into understanding. Even when you consciously reflect someone else's actions, it will feel natural. But don't force it, or it will come off that way. It's not a question of playing copycat. Simply stay aware of how you are authentically experiencing the situation, and allow your movements to reflect the engagement you feel.

Similarities Help Set the Mood

When meeting new people, the law of similarity tells us that we should be looking for commonalities or similarities to build trust, whatever and wherever those similarities might be. As we advance in our careers, our repertoire for dealing with new situations can narrow; it's important to keep broadening our approaches and tactics. Ask questions and be attuned to the wide variety of information you receive in response. The possible ways you may connect with someone are virtually endless, and by using the laws of curiosity and listening, you can discover what you have in common with someone and where your natural connections occur.

Commonalities create the foundations for trust when building new relationships. And just as it is important to seek out commonalities to help establish genuine ease in a conversation, it is crucial to end a conversation with those feelings of trust and ease intact. As we'll see in the next chapter, the lasting impression that an encounter creates is a powerful building block for likability and real relationships. I call it mood memory.

APPLYING THE LAW TO THE JOB HUNT

When it comes to hiring situations, the laws of similarity and association are the rules, not the exceptions. So when you are job hunting, think about the people you know *and* the people they know. If you've targeted certain companies to pursue, do you know any former or current employees who can help with an introduction? Or do any of your friends know former or current employees at the company? Alumni associations and social networking sites are useful tools for identifying and leveraging connections we might otherwise not take notice of. If you have the name of the person with whom you'll be interviewing, you can even plug it into a site such as LinkedIn to find out how you may already be connected, which can build context and create opportunities for conversation.

Sometimes the law of similarity acts in our favor without us having consciously put anything in motion. My colleague Walter related how he'd landed a client when the client recognized a former classmate of hers who'd given a testimonial for Walter's website. The client hadn't known the classmate well, but she had positive memories of him and decided by association that Walter's services must be first-rate.

If you can't identify a related person to help you access the company, how about an affiliated organization or firm? Does the company work with specific recruiting firms? What conferences do its employees go to, and can you attend one? Don't overlook the opportunity to highlight possible similarities on your résumé. That "Other Interests" section may have been just a space filler after college, but it's actually the perfect place to list hobbies or pursuits that you are passionate about and that may help you stand out. You need a place for the conversation to start in order to uncover commonalities, and it's up to you to create the opportunities for finding them.

Refresh Your Memory

The Law of Similarity. People like people like them.

The Sublaw of Association. People trust the sources they know best. Being associated with one of those trusted sources often means that the trust will, by association, be transferred to you.

Uncover Connections. Look for common interests and backgrounds, shared experiences and beliefs, to find similarities that can help you build connections with other people.

Be a Mirror. When you are comfortable in a conversation and feeling engaged, communicate it by reflecting it with your body language. Don't force it, just follow your natural mirroring tendencies.

It's Not Always Obvious. Don't get stuck on the obvious differences. You never know what similarities are there for the finding.

8

The Law of Mood Memory

"Nothing helps a bad mood like spreading it around."
—Bill Watterson, cartoonist and creator of "Calvin & Hobbes"

Elaine, one of my roommates during college, always tried to be a great friend. She would go out of her way to do nice things, bringing me soup whenever I felt sick, checking up on me twice a day if I was going through a rough patch with a guy I was dating, and so on. I genuinely wanted to reciprocate, but somehow my attempts never seemed good enough for her. She had a very strict image of what a good friend was, how a good friend should act, and what a good friend needed to do. She was incredibly demanding of her friends and she expected them, unequivocally, to go as far out of their ways for her as she did for them.

She always let me know when I didn't live up to her expectations, to the point that it began to seem as if she was constantly judging me. I could feel her disappointment in me, and despite my best attempts I couldn't stop fumbling into trouble with her. A misstep that seemed innocuous in my mind would wind up deeply upsetting her. If I didn't call exactly when I said I would, she'd take it as a personal affront.

> After a while I realized that whenever I thought about her I
> got tense. The muscles in my neck would tighten and a knot in
> the pit of my stomach would form. I knew that I shouldn't be
> having such a strong negative reaction to someone I consid-
> ered a friend, but thinking about her literally put me in a bad
> mood. Her critical nature and extremely high demands eventu-
> ally outweighed any enjoyment I got out of spending time with
> her, and our friendship deteriorated.

Think about your best friend and the last time you hung out and
had fun. Set that image in your mind and replay it in your head.
How does it make you feel? Are you mentally and maybe even
physically smiling? Now think about a recent conversation that
didn't go so well. Maybe you got trapped talking to someone
annoying at a bar, or you were cornered at the office by the colleague who has a knack for grousing about everything. Think
about having to talk to that person. How does the memory of that
situation make you feel? What does it feel like to imagine having
more conversations with that person?

The way you experience a person or a situation—the *feeling*
you get, whether negative or positive—lingers long after the actual
moment of interaction has past. The impressions you are left with
form the feelings you associate with that person or event. This is
called "mood memory." Creating positive mood memories of
yourself for other people is an essential part of increasing your
likability.

It's Not What You Said

We've all had that sensation: You're thinking about someone and
feeling good, without really being able to say why. Was it the conversation? Perhaps, but you barely even remember what was said.

Was it the person's mannerisms or general outlook on things? You're just not sure. Without being able to put your finger on the reasons, you just feel good about it all. This taps into the *law of mood memory*: People are more apt to remember how you made them feel than what you said. The colleague who manages to put everyone at ease and joke naturally without being a wise guy usually leaves everybody in a positive mood. But the peer who regularly dismisses your ideas and talks over you in meetings, well, thinking of that person can make you want to scowl and roll your eyes.

According to research, when we record a memory it is encoded not only with sensory data but with our mood and emotional state as well.[1] That's why when we recall a memory we often find ourselves reliving the feelings we had when it first occurred. The lingering remembrance of feeling—the mood memory—is an ingredient of likability. If other people have a positive mood memory of you, they are more likely to want to interact with you again.

LIVE THE LAW: *ELIMINATE THE NEGATIVE*

We often aren't aware of the moods we create. Just as it is important to understand how to create positive moods, it's crucial to understand how to stop making bad ones. Creating negative mood memory reduces your chances that the other person will actively seek out interacting with you again. To avoid doing the things that may make someone feel bad, you must increase your awareness of other people's and your own behavior.

First, make a list of the things that other people do that leave you feeling less than stellar. Did a friend answer his cell phone while you were in the middle of a story? Was a new acquaintance looking around the room instead of at you while you were talking?

Do you have a coworker who is always spinning out a worst-case scenario? Is there someone in your life who expresses things with such know-it-all confidence that she leaves little room for other people's opinions?

Once you've compiled the list, do some self-reflection. Are you prone to doing any of the things on that list? Has anyone ever given you feedback about something you've done that has left a negative impression?

Start another list of those things you may do to create negative mood memory. Don't worry too much if there are things you're doing that you're not aware of yet; just note the behaviors you can recognize, and remember—if someone does something that makes you feel bad, chances are you are making someone else feel bad if you do that, too. Choose one or two things from this list to start paying attention to and weeding out from your own behavior. Don't go crazy and choose too many at first, because you'll never be able to stay aware of all of them at once. Instead, choose a few so that you can truly focus on changing those behaviors.

Create Good Vibrations: Apply Other Laws

In many ways, mood memory is the culmination of the other laws we've learned so far. When you use what you know about how to increase your likability, you help create positive mood memories for other people while heightening your awareness of the impressions you leave those people with.

Let's review how, when used to their best effect, the laws of likability allow you to connect with other people in positive ways, thereby creating positive mood memories.

Harness Your Words, Your Body, and Your Energy

In Chapters 2, 3, and 4, we looked at how word choice, body language, and energy impact not just our perceptions of ourselves, but the perceptions others have of us. These laws intertwine to help shape mood memory. The energy with which you enter a situation dictates your word choices and body language. These things transmit your energy to other people, which in turn impacts their mood memory of you and the situation. It is a cycle, and one that you can consciously affect when you have awareness.

Choose Your Words

As we learned in Chapter 2, the words we use—in our heads and when we speak with other people—are a choice, and they reflect the ways we think. Positive framing can help us stay true to our authentic thoughts while giving us the opportunity to cast them in a positive light. Be aware of the words you are choosing, and keep asking yourself, "How can I look at this person, situation, or event positively?" Or, as I like to say, "What's the upside?"

I didn't have the easiest childhood. That statement alone is an example of choosing positive language. I could have said, "I had a difficult childhood," which would essentially be synonymous with the previous statement, but there is an important difference between the two ways of framing the basic fact. By choosing to say it wasn't the easiest childhood, I make it possible for the next thought to be, "But it wasn't the hardest childhood, either." Framing the situation this way immediately directs my thinking to the positive and balances my energy so that it's more neutral.

Mood memory does not apply only to people; it may also be attached to situations, events, and even companies and organizations. Because I was able to choose my words and use positive framing, my mood memory of my parents' divorce did not have disastrous results. I didn't attach a negative mood memory to the idea of marriage, and I didn't run screaming in the opposite direction away from commitment. I was able to focus on what the experience taught me about what to do, and what not to do, in relationships. So I've been able to create positive associations with marriage and approach it with clarity.

It's All in Your Body

In Chapter 3 we looked at psychologist Albert Mehrabian's likability formula, which states that body language contributes more than 50 percent to our overall likability. If you want the authentic you to stay with someone after the conversation is through, you need to be sure that what you say during the interaction is congruent with *how* you say it. Your verbal and nonverbal messages need to communicate the same things.

Body language has any number of subtleties. The variables of culture, gender, and style differences make it impossible for there to be hard-and-fast rules about nonverbal communication. Still, there are some basic ways we communicate through our gestures that are important to pay attention to. If you want to increase the potential for creating positive mood memories, be mindful of four aspects of body language:

◆ **Eye Contact.** Consistent eye contact makes a person feel listened to and respected, and therefore good. There is abundant science that supports this claim. Direct eye contact releases feel-good endorphins, and the heart starts to beat a little faster.[2] This doesn't mean you should be staring relentlessly at someone, of course. Follow your natural instincts to sustain eye contact in a way that communicates that you are listening to and comprehending what the other person is saying.

◆ **Smiling.** A genuine smile is incredibly powerful. It communicates ease and openness, approachability and trustworthiness. It is perhaps the single most immediate way to express likability. An authentic smile creates strong positive mood memories: Even if the other person doesn't remember what you've said, he may very well remember your smile. A smile is like an invitation to join a conversation and feel comfortable saying what is on your mind. Granted, some of us are not natural smilers, but I encourage you to practice. Eventually muscle memory will take over and you'll find yourself smiling more naturally. And I bet you'll feel happier, too.

◆ **Nodding.** The nod is another powerful nonverbal signal, but it can also be a bit of a gender-specific quandary. Numerous researchers, including productivity-management expert and author Simma Lieberman, posit that men nod when they agree with something, and women nod to indicate that they are listening. The best tack, whether you are a man or a woman and regardless of how and why you nod, is to be aware of how much you are doing it. Nodding should be a signal that's in your nonverbal toolbox. You don't want to overuse it, because its purpose—to indicate agreement or attentiveness—can be diminished if it's done too much. By the same token, pay attention to when the nod might actually help you convey how you are experiencing the situation. Especially when backed up by quick verbal signals ("Hmm, that's interesting," or "I couldn't agree with you more"), nodding can effectively communicate that you comprehend what you're hearing.

◆ **Personal Space.** The physical distance between two people when they are talking is referred to as personal space, and there are two main things that tend to influence how someone feels about it: culture and communication style. Some cultures are more comfortable with intimate personal space, others prefer to maintain more distance, and it all depends upon the situation. If you travel to the Middle East, you'll see groups of male friends walking together, arms draped around one another's shoulders. Men who are walking down the street with their male friends in Northern Europe usually stand a bit apart. The communication styles we learned about in Chapter 3 also impact personal-space preferences: Zig Zags and Circles are often fine with the touched shoulder to indicate emphasis; Angles and Straight Lines, however, like to maintain nonvisible, no-touch boundaries. Keep cultural and communication-style differences in mind when it comes to handling personal space, and trust your own instincts. Whatever feels natural and right for you, as you stay aware of the situation you're in and the person you are with, is what determines the best course of action.

Shift Your Energy

Chapter 4 explored the law of energy: It's contagious. If you want to make others feel good, start by feeling good yourself. As was emphasized in that chapter, feeling good doesn't necessarily mean feeling perky and happy; it means connecting with what feels positive and appropriate in the situation and the person you're dealing with.

If you know that, going into a situation, you are not in a pleasant place mentally, make the choice to shift your energy. Think about what energy *would* work best for you in that moment, and if necessary, remember a time when you did have that energy. Focus on as many details as you can to recall what it felt like, and absorb it. The idea is not to fake the mood, but rather to find or re-create the mood within yourself instead.

Admire, Appreciate, and Ask for Advice

Curiosity and listening can have a profound positive impact on the connections we make. They also are powerful tools for shaping positive mood memory. Use the tactics you learned in Chapter 5 about curiosity and in Chapter 6 on listening to create good energy and lasting impressions when forming connections.

Don't Just Think It—Say It

Chapter 6's "just say it" strategy for managing internal distractions and increasing listening capacity has direct application for creating mood memory. The basic premise is: Don't let people misinterpret what's going on in your mind when you can just tell them. In the context of mood memory, the phrase becomes, "Don't just think it—say it."

In my own life, an experience that made me get proactive about my own mood-memory awareness was when my colleague Laurie had breast cancer. Even though we weren't particularly close, when I saw how she faced her illness with such grace, courage, and humor, I had to say something, even if I embarrassed myself and her. So I finally told her how in awe of her I felt. She was deeply touched, and shared with me that cancer had taken so much from her but given her so much too, and that my kind words were one of those gifts. Her perspective humbled me. Soon after that, she passed away. I think of her and I am reminded of how short life can be, and of how we mustn't waste the opportunities we have to say what we want and need to say.

In life-and-death situations, we often remember to put words to what we are thinking. My experience with Laurie reminded me that I needed to do the same in less momentous situations as well. It was like waking up from a daze. I started consciously engaging people even in small moments, telling them what I was thinking when it was appropriate, putting words of appreciation and admiration to the thoughts that had previously stayed in my head. I thanked the bus driver who waited for me while I ran to catch the bus, not with the usual perfunctory "Thanks," but by looking him in the eye and letting him know that I appreciated his kindness and that it mattered to me, saying something more engaging and personable such as, "You made my day and saved me from the wrath of a very punctual boss." I stopped to chat with and thank the doorman who was always there with a smile and a hello, helping me with my packages, kids, or a neighbor's dog. I went up to the speaker at a meeting I attended to compliment him on handling a heckler in an effective but courteous manner.

The key is to open ourselves up to seeing the good things that are always around us and that we rarely stop to notice, appreciate, or give thanks for. *Don't just think it—say it.*

Not long ago I was conducting a two-week training session at a manufacturing company, and we were discussing employee evaluations. One of the participants was talking about the annual review as a chance to "get yourself into the conversation." It was such a great phrase and such a great way of framing the situation that I immediately complimented him on it and used the phrase for the rest of the training, giving him credit every time I referenced it. Not only did this make him feel good, but it made the entire group feel engaged: They were proud that one of their members had coined a phrase I wanted to incorporate in my training, and they felt as if they were truly active participants in the sessions.

Telling people what you genuinely admire about them can increase the connection they have with you; it makes the other person feel understood. The more connections we make with someone, the more likely that those connections will build into a meaningful relationship.

LIVE THE LAW: *DON'T JUST THINK IT—SAY IT*

Actively noticing the things you admire about other people, and telling them so, may seem like a small gesture, but it can have a big impact. People you know and even strangers appreciate genuine compliments and praise because it makes them feel valued. The things you remark upon do not have to be momentous; they can be as simple as how someone always answers the phone with a smile in his voice, or as important as how someone handles a difficult situation. If your admiration is sincere, the compliment will be genuinely appreciated, and articulating it will make you feel good, too.

OPTION 1: APPRECIATE SOMEONE YOU KNOW

Think about the people you see on a regular basis, and the things you admire about them. Perhaps you admire how diligently the receptionist at your office keeps everything running on time, or you're impressed by how a colleague always seems to close even the toughest deals. Now put words to those thoughts of admiration. The next time they demonstrate the behavior you admire, tell them. Articulating your appreciation not only increases positive mood memory, it may also open up the chance for you to engage them more about their likable trait and learn from what they do.

OPTION 2: MAKE A STRANGER'S DAY

Complimenting people we don't know may feel strange, but we all have ample opportunities for doing this in a natural way, and making a habit of it further raises our awareness of the situations we are in and the mood memories we create. The next time you are traveling and experience flight disruptions that provoke cranky customers to vent on a calm, gracious flight attendant, let the flight attendant know he's doing a great job. When faced with one of those maddening customer service problems that can keep you on the phone, frustrated, for what feels like hours, remember to tell the extremely patient employee on the other end that you know the problem isn't her fault, and thank her for her help.

Take It to the Next Level: Seek Advice

Expressing your genuine interest in someone by following your curiosity can build connections and open an avenue for deeper bonds. To maximize the law of curiosity (Chapter 5) in creating mood memory, seek out advice from those people you truly admire and hold in high regard. When you ask for someone's opinion, advice, or expertise, the message you are sending is: *I value you.* This creates positive mood memory because people generally feel respected and recognized for their strengths when someone else seeks advice from them; at the same time, you are leveraging your curiosity and creating opportunities to learn. Asking for advice may leave you feeling vulnerable, but this can be a good thing: Being vulnerable is being open and authentic, which are very likable qualities. By having the courage to expose yourself, you open up the door for ongoing communication.

In professional situations, the mentor/mentee relationship is a classic advice-seeking dynamic. This relationship can be effectively cultivated with someone already in your life, but it can also be set in motion with people you are meeting for the first time. One time I found myself sitting next to a woman named Ora, an adjunct professor at NYU, during a conference lunch break. Ever since I was a kid, I'd dreamed about being a college professor one day, but never wanted to do it full-time. I asked Ora how she got started at NYU. As I raptly listened to her story, she asked me if I'd ever done any teaching. I explained that it was something I'd always hoped to do, part-time, but wasn't sure how to pursue. She offered to introduce me to the head of her department, and came through with the introduction when I followed up later that week. During the next several weeks she generously offered her time and advice as I reached out to the department chair and set up an interview. Thanks in large part to her guidance, I began an adjunct position at NYU the next semester, and Ora continued to help me navigate the exciting new challenges the experience presented.

Don't worry that as a mentee you may feel as if you are taking more than you are giving. You will inevitably get your chance to be in the giving role (we'll take a closer look at the law of giving in Chapter 10). Also, remember that people like to be valued and recognized for their expertise. By seeking advice, you create positive mood memory, which helps sustain the relationship so that it can continue to evolve.

Know When It Is Over

Knowing when to end a conversation is often a challenge. Ending it too quickly can send the signal that you are losing interest, or would rather be talking to someone else, or any number of negative things that will leave the person you're conversing with feeling bad. Dragging it out too long, though, can create the impression that you want to monopolize the other person's time or are oblivious to the subtle wrap-it-up hints the other person may be giving.

You want to leave a conversation with the other person wanting a little bit more of you and feeling positively energized from having interacted with you. If you could read people's minds as you are exiting the conversation, ideally they'd be thinking something like this:

- "It was great speaking with you; I can't wait for our next chance to talk."
- "It was terrific that you asked me for my advice. It gave me a chance to help, and it made me feel smart."
- "You have an excellent handshake, and your eye contact was confident and engaging the whole time we were talking. I know you were paying attention and were really interested in what I was saying."

When you're not sure if you should end the conversation, try one of the following conversation curtailers; they leave a door open if the person you are speaking with wants to continue the conversation but also provide an out if the other person feels it's time to wrap things up.

- ◆ **"The more the merrier. . . ."** If you spot someone not engaged in conversation, suggest bringing them into yours. Adding a new person to the group can refresh the conversation and allow people the chance to exit gracefully if they want to.

- ◆ **"Can I get you a drink?"** This comment creates an easy exit if one is wanted. Saying, "I am going to grab a drink, can I get you one?" allows for both possibilities—the exit or the continuation. Take your cue from the person's response.

- ◆ **"I'm headed this way."** This tactic can be particularly useful in a conference or workshop setting. Try saying, "I wanted to go check out the (fill in the blank), would you like to join me?" It shows that you are not just trying to get rid of the other person, and that you'd even welcome the chance to explore more of the event with him.

- ◆ **"Shall we mingle?"** This is similar to the previous option, but applicable to almost any social situation. Moving through a crowd with someone also creates opportunities to reenergize a previous conversation or open up new topics of discussion.

Before closing a conversation, strive to (1) make the other person feel good, and (2) create an opportunity to follow up. We'll look at the follow-up component in the next section of the book. But in terms of ending the conversation with positive mood memory, if you are doing your best and find that it just isn't happening in a given situation, let it go. It's better to exit a less-than-stellar conversation gracefully, creating neutral mood memory, than to try forcing the issue to such an extent that the other person remembers the interaction negatively. Exiting the situation with a neutral impression leaves the door open to trying to connect again in the future.

Most conversations end naturally, with or without the aid of a conversation curtailer. For those instances when it's clear that it's time to bring things to a close but somehow the moment still feels awkward, use one of these "back pocket" conversation closers. Pair your words with body language that reinforces the verbal indication that the conversation is concluding, such as putting on your coat or picking up your bag, shifting your body toward the exit, and extending your arm to shake hands. People always understand the need to exit the conversation if you say:

- "I will make sure to (fill in the follow-up item)."
- "Do you prefer phone or e-mail? Great, you will hear from me very soon."
- "I am so glad I met you. Thanks for telling me about. . . ."
- "Do you know where the restrooms are?"

Leave Them Feeling Good

In essence, the law of mood memory is about creating a feel-good association so that you leave someone else with a favorable impression of you. There are many ways to increase the probability of good mood memory. But the most important of all is: Be authentic.

THE CORPORATE APPLICATION

Mood memory is fundamental to the success—or failure—of corporations. How a business is run, how it deals with its customers and treats its employees, has everything to do with how it is perceived, and how people choose to interact with that business based on what they remember from previous experiences.

How you feel about your Internet provider or local hardware store or any provider of goods or services has been shaped by your experiences with that entity, especially the personnel with whom you've interacted and the quality of services provided. If you have positive mood memories of those experiences, you are apt to go back and even recommend them to others. If not, there's almost always another retailer or carrier who can offer you similar goods or services.

There are stores I seek out because shopping there is consistently a positive experience. I know they will stand by their products, be pleasant on the phone, and make any transactions easy. I love that when I walk into my local Restoration Hardware store I know every associate by name, and they all recognize me. But even when I first started shopping there, before I'd even purchased a single item, the staff was welcoming and friendly, and never pushy. Even when the sales associates are busy with other customers, they keep you updated about when someone will be free to assist you. This past holiday season, the lines were long and I was having a tough time choosing colors for the items I wanted. Chaz, the assistant manager, suggested that once I made my decision on colors, I could go home and then call them to place my order, and pay over the phone, which I did. When I went back the next day, he had the items all packaged up for me and ready to go. This is just one example of how the store staff continually go out of their way to provide top-notch service. And so I happily keep shopping there.

But in the corporate world, customer loyalty isn't enough. To be truly successful companies must master employee allegiance. One tell-tale way they display this, particularly noteworthy as of late, is how they handle layoffs. My friend Edward was working for several years at a company he really liked. He was in a small division, and in hindsight he admits that he was oblivious to the division's dwindling importance within the company, but he and his team worked well together and were highly effective, and overall his experience of working for the company was extremely positive.

Then came the layoffs. HR put dozens of employees—including everyone in Edward's division—into a room and made them wait for hours until, one by one, employees were told they were getting laid off. They got one day to evacuate the office, with a minimal severance package. When Edward went to tell some of his colleagues in other divisions his news, a company partner followed him suspiciously and asked where he was going, as if he were about to steal trade secrets. Needless to say, the poor way the layoffs were handled completely erased any positive feelings Edward previously had about the company.

On the flip side of the coin, my friend Monica, who is in the same industry as Edward, got laid off right around the same time. She got six times the severance he did, as well as outplacement services, and full use of the office and office equipment during her search for a new job. The company that was letting her go supported her in her search because it understood that a former employee might one day be a future client, and the company wisely didn't want to burn any bridges.

Refresh Your Memory

The Law of Mood Memory. People are more apt to remember how you made them feel than what you said.

It's Not What You Say, It's How You Say It. The overall energy you impart often has more of a lasting impression on someone than the specifics of what you said.

Harness Your Words, Your Body, and Your Energy. The same strategies for word choice (Chapter 2), body language (Chapter 3), and shifting energy (Chapter 4) can be applied to creating positive mood memory. How you perceive of and present yourself directly impacts the impression you leave.

Admire, Appreciate, and Ask for Advice. Articulating what you admire about other people makes them feel understood; asking for advice makes them feel valued and shows that you can be vulnerable, which fosters trust. All are powerful tools for creating positive mood memory.

Know When It's Over. Exit the conversation at the appropriate time to ensure the most positive mood memory and the best opportunities for productively following up.

Part C

■

After the Conversation:
Build Relationships

Two years ago one of my clients, Pete, a software designer, was at a barbecue hosted by the alumni group of his wife's alma mater. He got to chatting with Henry, one of his wife's classmates. Henry is in the technology industry too, and Pete knew him socially. The two of them always had a lot to casually talk about when they saw one another.

A few weeks after the barbecue, Pete's wife ran into Henry, who mentioned that there was a position opening up at his company. She suggested to Pete that he follow up with Henry about the job, but Pete was hesitant. He wasn't crazy about his job but he was satisfied enough with it, and he didn't want Henry to think he was imposing or being presumptuous. At his wife's gentle nudging Pete finally did reach out to Henry, and interviewed for the position. He landed the job, which he's thrilled with. Today Pete chairs an industry association of software designers that Henry is also a part of, and the two frequently collaborate on projects for their company and the organization.

Once you've had the initial conversation, and perhaps even multiple interactions, and established an authentic connection based on likability, what happens next? How do you move past the handshake or the friendly industry chitchat over burgers and beers at a barbecue?

This section is about how to maintain contact so that there continue to be opportunities for our connections to flourish and grow. It can be easy to brush off what happens after the conversation. We may feel as if we don't have a reason to reach out, or have nothing substantive to say to the person in a follow-up message, or we're simply too swamped to take the time to do it. But following up is a key part of building meaningful relationships. In the next three chapters we'll learn effective methods for staying in someone's mind, following up on the conversation, offering value, and inevitably learning how to be patient. Transforming an acquaintance into a relationship takes time.

9

The Law of Familiarity

"In politics, familiarity doesn't breed contempt. It breeds votes."

—Paul Lazarsfeld, sociologist

The first time I heard about Mark, I was in desperate need of a consultant who could design a corporate training program for a rush project set to launch in less than two weeks. I had a new business and was working on a project for only my second client, and I needed help pulling it together, fast. I put out feelers and all roads led to Mark. After the two of us talked a few times to get acquainted and discuss the project, I hired his firm for the assignment. I also joined his e-mail list and began getting his weekly messages that contained inspiring quotes and ideas for staying motivated.

Over the coming months we had little direct contact, yet it seemed that whenever I met someone in my new field and we played the name game, Mark's name came up. Everyone seemed to know him.

More than a year after our initial introduction, and out of the blue, I received a congratulatory e-mail from Mark. I had been quoted in the *New York Times* and he had seen it. I was really excited to receive the e-mail, and appreciated his effort to reach out to me. Months later, after my business started to gather momentum, one of my clients, wanting to expand its coaching platform, asked me to bring even more consultants on board. Mark's name immediately popped into mind, and he was the first person I introduced to the client.

Mark and I have continued to stay on one another's radar screens over the years. When we were both writing book proposals, we touched base and compared notes. Every once in a while I receive an e-mail from him, announcing an appearance on NPR or CNN.

Although our direct contact is infrequent, Mark is never too far from my mind. He has managed to get his name out there in so many effective ways that it keeps coming up with the kind of frequency that instills familiarity and credibility.

Early in my career, I was trying to get a foot in the door at a major bank. I met an employee there named Roberto, who passed along the name and contact information of the training-department head, Kristi, and said I should use his name when I reached out to her. I did so, but got no response. A friend and former co-worker was also working at the bank, and several months earlier had offered to pass along my name if I ever wanted him to. I decided that the time had come to take him up on his offer. He e-introduced Kristi and me, and this time I heard back from her almost immediately. She said, "I have been hearing your name all over the place." Apparently my name also came up in an HR forum that she was a part of. It wasn't until she'd heard my name from multiple sources that she e-mailed me back.

I believe it was only because my name was mentioned several times that Kristi started to build some trust in me. This is a regularly occurring phenomenon. "Oh, I've heard of her before," goes the thinking, "she must be good." The more that people hear from you or about you, the more they will develop feelings of trust in you, and the more their comfort with you will grow. Creating mental and physical familiarity enhances likability, and it's important to develop this quality whether you are in or out of sight of the other person.

People Like Who and What They Know

I was at a conference once and noticed a man whose name tag identified him as being with a company that sounded very familiar to me. I quickly searched the company name on my BlackBerry to jog my memory. Then I went up to the man to introduce myself, mentioning the name of the partner I knew at his firm (the law of similarity on my side). He seemed only lukewarm to my efforts, so after a brief conversation I didn't push it further. I sent him a follow-up e-mail after the event and got a brief reply.

About six weeks later we ended up at another conference together, and this time we were introduced by a mutual friend. He was a bit friendlier than he'd been when we first met, and he remembered our earlier encounter, but he still maintained his distance and didn't reciprocate my effort to deepen the connection. Over the next few months our paths continued to cross, and each time we ran into one another he'd be a bit warmer. By the time we ended up speaking on the same panel a year later, he was all smiles. It was the *law of familiarity* in action: People feel comfortable with who and what they know.

The man took a long time to let his relaxed, warm side come through. It's not uncommon for people to warm up to new acquaintances in stages, building that warmth of engagement over time. At first, I was an unknown entity. And even though we had a common friend, he needed more of a connection for there to be trust and comfort between us. People tend to be most comfortable with the people and things they are familiar with.

Advertising executives bank on this concept all the time. The more that consumers hear about a brand, the more comfortable they become with it, the more they trust it, and the more validity the brand has. Think about Super Bowl commercials: Why are advertisers willing to pay a million dollars to run a spot during the show? The answer is that so many viewers will be watching the Super Bowl and the commercials generate so much postshow buzz that even the names of companies with mediocre commercials will be mentioned again and again, increasing familiarity.

There is, of course, a fine line between keeping your name in people's minds by building positive associations, and barraging them to such an extent that they tune you out. The key is to build familiarity in an authentic way. Authenticity, as we've seen, applies across the board with likability. Reach out in the spirit of connection, not in a narcissistic attempt at blatant self-promotion.

Remember Me?

As always, the laws of likability build on one another. After you have already fostered connections and initiated familiarity with someone during an interaction, you can continue to develop that familiarity when the encounter is over. Once you've met and decided that you like a person, and established a great mood memory, that's precisely the time you want to stay in touch and sustain the conversation.

There are obvious instances where it's clear that we can and should follow up. Even more critical, though, is to increase our frequency of reaching out. When we regularly extend ourselves, in a variety of ways and for a variety of reasons, we allow connections to continue unfolding, which strengthens familiarity and likability. Each time you reach out to another person, employ language that fosters positive mood memory; even stating something as simple as "we" in your follow-up reinforces the connection.

Congratulations

Sending a note of congratulations or well wishes is a simple and unobtrusive way to stay in someone's mind, increase positive feelings, and express your interest in maintaining a connection. The topic you mention is less important than the real message you are sending, which is, "I was listening and I am thinking about you."

To find your topic, think back to your conversation. What did you learn about the person? What were you talking about? Your follow-up needs to show that you were paying attention to what the person was saying and picked up on significant experiences or milestones that the person was sharing. You want to demonstrate that you not only heard but also listened to what was being said.

Here is just a short list of some of the things I may learn about someone during a conversation and that could become part of my follow-up communications later:

- Upcoming work event, client meeting, training, conference, or workshop
- Alma mater or favorite sports team's recent game or newsworthy event
- Upcoming vacation destination or staycation plans
- Battling an illness/aiding a sick parent, spouse, friend, or child
- New baby arrived or on the way; announcement of whether it's a boy or a girl
- The person's own birthday or child's birthday; plans to attend or throw a birthday party

If you tend to be fuzzy on the details after talking with someone new, do what I do immediately after walking away from a new acquaintance: Jot down notes. I carry a pen with me at all times so that I can flip over a business card and write down a few comments about how I met the person, what we talked about, and any particular information I may have learned that I want to remember. This strategy can be especially useful when you're attending a networking event or a conference and you may leave with a pile of cards in your pocket (and after having had a few cocktails that blur your memory).

Sometimes I'll even make a note of what a person looked like to help me with recall, though an excellent Outlook search tool called Xobni ("inbox" spelled backward) has helped me all but eliminate the need to do this, since it displays photos of my e-mail contacts. There are all sorts of electronic resources that can help you keep up with people and determine the right times to reach out with a congratulatory note. And these notes don't have to be specifically about the person: They might be in reference to news about the person's company closing a major deal, acquiring an interesting client, or bringing a new CEO on board.

Don't worry that the topic you settle on might be unrelated to your common interest, or even if it refers to a small detail that was part of a much larger conversation. Following up with a congratulatory message is a simple way to show other people that you were thinking of them, and it increases familiarity and the positive mood memory associated with your shared connection. Not long ago I received an e-mail from a former student, congratulating me on a mention she'd seen of me in *Real Simple* magazine. It was an unexpected forum for us to reconnect through, but it was great to hear from her and be back in touch, and I was glad to see that she was putting the law of familiarity into action.

LIVE THE LAW: *HARNESS TECHNOLOGY*

Use technology to stay updated about what's going on in people's lives. Here are two valuable resources.

DOWNLOAD XOBNI

Xobni is an ingenious e-mail application for users of PCs and BlackBerrys that I find absolutely invaluable. You can download the free version at www.xobni.com. Xobni creates a sidebar in your inbox window that makes searching your inbox and finding information about contacts fast and easy. There are three particular Xobni features that I've come to especially value:

1. **The Visual Component.** If you receive an e-mail from someone who is also on Facebook, Twitter, or LinkedIn, their profile pictures from those applications will appear in your Xobni sidebar. So many of my initial connections with people happen through e-mail or over the phone, so if I can see their picture before we meet face-to-face, I can get a better sense of their age and how I might find commonalities with them. And putting a face to the voice increases my familiarity with a person.

2. **Linking Online.** If it turns out that a new e-mail contact uses Facebook, Twitter, or LinkedIn, Xobni gives me the option to quickly and easily connect with the person on these social networking sites. That additional follow-up connection increases familiarity and the potential for future interactions.

3. **Establishing Connections.** Even if you are not yet using social networking sites, Xobni lets you see an e-mail contact's network, so you can quickly get a sense of how you may be connected. This gives you further opportunities and topics for continuing the conversation, and for leveraging the laws of similarity and association.

SET UP GOOGLE ALERTS

Remember Mark, the master of familiarity? He has a terrific method for keeping up with the goings-on of friends, colleagues, and their companies: He uses Google Alerts.

Setting up a Google Alert for someone or something is extremely straightforward. You enter whatever it is you want to use as the search terms—someone's name, a company name, or even an industry term. You then choose (from a drop-down menu) where you want to search for it: in News, Blogs, Web, Video, Discussion Groups, or all of the above. You select the frequency and number of hits you want to receive, then enter your e-mail address, and voilà. The information you want to track is delivered directly to your inbox.

Your challenge: Set up at least one Google Alert before finishing this book.

Go to www.google.com/alerts to initiate a search.

Social Networking

The Internet has made creating familiarity with someone infinitely easier. Social networking sites such as Facebook, LinkedIn, and Twitter are great resources for staying in touch in numerous ways. Sending an invitation to connect through one of these sites is an excellent way to contact a new associate without having to find a reason for the interaction. You can time the invitation for immediately after your initial meeting, or wait a few weeks and send it as a way to touch base.

Different people use the various sites in different ways. For example, many people prefer to use Facebook for personal relationships and LinkedIn for business associations. Find the approach that feels natural for you, and build your connections to increase your familiarity.

Facebook

Facebook is a pure social networking site with no other agenda than to provide a forum for people to connect and be friends. It is an amazing vehicle for reconnecting with old acquaintances, rekindling forgotten friendships, and helping to establish new connections. And its reach is phenomenal. According to 2010 statistics, almost 42 percent of the entire U.S. population has a Facebook account,[1] and weekly tracking figures reveal that traffic to Facebook often outstrips traffic to Google.[2]

Each user's profile includes such information as personal interests, hobbies, birthday, relationship status, and photos, so Facebook is a great venue for discovering further points of similarity with someone.

It's also an excellent tool for staying in someone's mind in a friendly, unobtrusive way. You can respond to other people's status updates, joining in on whatever conversation has been sparked, and you can post messages directly to people's profile pages, or "walls." You can use your own status updates to generate conversations, too. Sharing a link to a funny article, asking for advice about a particular problem, making a comment about current events—these are all common ways that people initiate back-and-forths with their connections and maintain a presence on Facebook. The key, of course, is not to post too much or too often: You want to use the tool to create dialogues with your Facebook friends, not subject them to your running monologue.

You can also utilize the chat feature, essentially Facebook's instant messaging system. Ping people with a quick "Hello!" when you are both logged in at the same time. It's warm and friendly but simple, and it doesn't impose. In addition to connecting with acquaintances and friends, you can join groups and networks that help people to connect around a particular event, shared passion, or past affiliation. A reunion for the summer camp I attended as a child was organized through the camp's Facebook page. If not for Facebook I never would have reconnected with most of the people I saw at the event, and yet now I'm socializing and working with several of them.

LinkedIn

LinkedIn is a business-oriented social networking site for making professional connections. The information listed in a LinkedIn profile is intended strictly for professional use, and you have full control over all the content that relates to you. You can share information about the work you are doing and upcoming events you are attending or hosting, join or create networking groups, provide and receive professional references, and expand your network through "warm" introductions, or e-connections made through a mutual contact.

According to its website, as of January 2011, LinkedIn had more than 90 million registered users across more than 200 countries and territories worldwide. There is an immediate level of trust and connection conveyed with LinkedIn, since the site uses a "gated access" approach; that is, requesting a network connection with someone requires a preexisting relationship or shared contact. I rarely get LinkedIn requests from random people, and I never get spammed by it.

The simple act of updating your LinkedIn profile can keep

your name in front of people, since this activity appears in the weekly updates they receive. I always read the weekly notifications e-mail I get from LinkedIn. It lets me know quickly and easily which members of my network have been active on the site, and how. What I do next depends on what I've learned.

◆ **Status Updates.** I respond to these notices as I would to a post on Facebook; in other words, I reply only if I have something to say about what's been posted. If a connection is sharing a notice about an upcoming event, I may wish him luck or ask for more information about it.

◆ **New Connections.** I check them out to see if anyone in my network has connected with someone I know. If I know the people but am not yet connected to them, I may send a connection request. And if I'm surprised by the connection between two people I know, I may e-mail them both to find out how they're associated, thus strengthening the circles of connection and creating opportunities to share information.

◆ **People Joining Groups.** These notifications are my way of finding out about groups I may want to join. If one of my connections has joined a group that sounds intriguing, I may e-mail the person to see if she is finding the group useful.

◆ **Answering or Asking a Question.** As a LinkedIn user, you can reply to the discussion forums when there is an existing conversation you want to weigh in on. You can also initiate a forum discussion when you have something you want to query your connections about.

◆ **New Job Positions.** When I see that a connection has a new job title, I always send a congratulatory e-mail. It's a way to inquire about the new position and to find out what someone has been up to. People usually love to share their stories. Let the law of curiosity take over, and reach out with an inquiry.

Twitter

Twitter is sometimes described as the short message service (SMS) of the Internet because the site lets people communicate with micro-messages of 140 characters or fewer. According to the Twitter website, as of March 2011, there were more than 175 million Twitter users, and more than 95 million tweets (i.e., Twitter messages) were issued each day.

One of the most interesting things about Twitter is that, while it's possible to keep your Twitter network restricted so that you have to approve "followers" before they can see your tweets, the vast majority of people and companies using it keep their networks open, so you can follow anyone or anything, from Joe Schmo to JetBlue, and hear what they're saying. National politicians, Fortune 500 CEOs, and top journalists are all among the ranks of active Twitter users, and by following them, you become part of their conversations.

Another benefit to the general open-door ethos of Twitter is that it can be a way to form new connections. As I was writing this chapter, I logged in to my Twitter account, posted a tweet, and within seconds received an e-mail that I had a new follower. Some people are even using Twitter to stage distinctly twenty-first-century get-togethers. Lance Armstrong, who has more than 2 million Twitter followers, created a scene in the summer of 2009 when he was in Scotland and tweeted, "Hey Glasgow, Scotland! I'm coming your way tomorrow. Who wants to go for a bike ride?" Hundreds of people showed up in response, and spent the day biking along with Armstrong and connecting with one another.

Twitter updates inform you of what the people in your network are doing, seeing, thinking, or reading. Many times a stream of tweets will be purely informational, but it's also possible to turn them into a dialogue. Whenever Tim Ferriss, author of *The 4-Hour Workweek*, travels, he tweets questions about the destination he is visiting and gets hundreds of tweets back in response. He says it's a great way to learn about a place from the local perspective and start a micro-conversation about it.

Although Twitter is particularly effective for people or companies with substantial followings, it can be useful even if you're not a well-known personality. My friend Sean is a Lego artist and author. He tweets about upcoming times and locations of book signings, or an exhibition of one of his pieces, or if an article or video about his work has recently been posted. It's his way of letting his followers keep up with what he's doing and when he's having special events, creating opportunities for connection and meeting up.

LIVE THE LAW: *LEARNING THE LINGO*

Facebook, LinkedIn, and Twitter are currently the three most popular social networking sites, but there are many others, and the landscape is changing all the time. Each site uses its own vocabulary and provides different benefits, restrictions, and features, though the basic terms and functionalities often bear similarities to one another. Here is a summary of the main terminology used in social networking, and how it varies between what are, at the moment, the three most heavily used sites.

Profile. Your profile is your online presence, which can also be thought of as your homepage. You have options for personalizing your profile, and you can choose to include as much or as little information as you want. You can add photos to your profile so that other people can put a face to your name. Privacy settings give you further control over who can access the information displayed in your profile. Each site requests different types of details for fleshing out your profile.

- A Facebook profile acts as a personalized journal/photo album/message board. Multiple sections allow for a great deal of customization of your profile. You can display your hometown, birthday, relationship status, contact information, work history, schools attended, photos from a recent trip, favorite movies, and on and on.

- A LinkedIn profile functions almost as an online résumé, with detailed information about your work history, education, interests, and group associations. Your profile also displays testimonials that your connections may have posted about your work—essentially online letters of reference.

- A Twitter profile is the least robust, simply displaying your name, location, web address, brief bio, the numbers of people you follow and who follow you, and a history of your tweets.

Person in Your Network. Your network consists of those people you accept into your online circle, and the people who accept you into theirs. Social networking sites use different terms to connote the member of a network. The terms are:

- Facebook "friend"

- LinkedIn "connection"

- Twitter "follower"

Updates. The "social networking" component of each site comes not just in the posted profile information, but in the real-time exchanges that can occur. Updates let you post a short note about what you are currently doing, thinking, or experiencing, and share it with your network. Many professionals use updates as a way to share information about events they are attending or hosting with colleagues and associates.

- Facebook uses the term "Status Update." Fill in the status field on your profile page and click the button to broadcast it to your Facebook friends.

- LinkedIn uses the term "Network Update." Post questions, thoughts, or article links via LinkedIn's homepage or through the update link on your own profile page.

- Twitter uses the term "Tweet." This is the essence of Twitter: anything you want to say, posted in 140 characters or fewer.

Notifications. You can create a setting so the site sends you up-to-the-minute messages when people in your network post an update or change their profile.

- Facebook allows you to pick and choose what information you want to receive and how you want to receive it. You set up your preferences to be notified when someone sends you a friend request, comments on your status update, or uploads a photo, for instance. These notifications can be sent via e-mail or text; smartphone apps give you access to Facebook while you're on the go.

- LinkedIn allows you to decide how often you want to receive notifications (immediately, daily, weekly) and what types of information (events, group activity, individual connections' activity) you want to be notified about. There are downloadable smartphone apps so that you can access the site on your mobile device.

- Twitter requires you to set up notifications individually for each person you are following; then you can arrange to be notified of new tweets by text or e-mail. There are numerous Twitter platforms for tweeting from your smartphone.

Wall. This is a term solely used by Facebook. Your profile wall is essentially a virtual message board. The people in your network—your Facebook "friends"—can post messages on your wall and comment on your photos, videos, or status updates. Bear in mind that it is not a private forum—anyone in your Facebook network can see what has been posted on your wall, and if mutual friends post things to one another's walls you'll see those messages, too.

Regards

The three most effective things I do to stay in people's minds are also the methods that feel the most natural and authentic, because they come from a genuine place: That is to say, they reflect the value I place on connections and building them. One of my methods is to introduce people I think should meet one another. I am the common link as these new relationships spark, and therefore I am front of mind. The second is to invite people to or inform them of upcoming events that they might find of interest. Even if none of us ends up attending the events, people will know that I was thinking of them, which will in turn prompt them to think of me.

The third thing I regularly do is to send my regards. It may seem trite to say, "Tell so and so I said hello," but it is an easy thing to do, and can even be helpful to the person conveying the message. It provides a ready topic of conversation, and gives people a chance to leverage the law of similarity.

Get Out There

Hearing someone's name mentioned again and again in positive contexts can build professional credibility and help establish comfortable rapport and ease. Creating familiarity doesn't require scheduled meetings or planned conversations, either. It can be done without having actual face time or giving the impression that you are hounding someone. By simply following up on shared details and harnessing electronic resources, it is possible to steadily create familiarity and associate your name with appropriate ideas and events. Remember to pursue these strategies in ways that feel true and authentic to you, and that aren't obtrusive or pushy. Don't get in someone's face, just be in their circle.

Refresh Your Memory

The Law of Familiarity. People feel comfortable with who and what they know.

Build Familiarity. Stay in someone's mind through social networking applications, notes of well wishing, personal recommendations, and sending your regards.

Continue the Conversation. Leverage technology and social networking sites to increase your opportunities to interact.

Keep It Authentic. Harness electronic media tools in ways that seem natural and true to you. Don't get in someone's face, just be in their circle.

10

The Law of Giving

"It is one of the most beautiful compensations of life, that no man can sincerely try to help another without helping himself."

—Ralph Waldo Emerson, nineteenth-century writer and philosopher

Just as I was getting ready to make the leap from the finance industry to starting my own business, I attended the Columbia Women in Business (CWIB) conference and sat in on a panel about entrepreneurship. As someone daunted by the thought of going out on my own, I found myself particularly interested in one panelist named Amy. She had already successfully launched a business very similar in structure and services to the one I was planning. On top of that, Amy was articulate and eloquent when speaking about the experience on the panel. I was immediately in awe of her and wanted to speak to her.

Rather than compete with everyone swarming the stage at the end of the session, I instead sought her out at lunch and effusively told her how impressed I was by her career path and her work. She smiled, genuinely honored by the compliment. We chatted for the rest of the lunch about some of the challenges she had faced when establishing her business.

By the end of lunch I was even more in awe of her and everything she'd done, and I decided to take a chance and ask her if she'd be willing to meet me for coffee one day soon to continue the conversation. She suggested that we meet for lunch instead. A week later we sat in a restaurant for three hours while she poured out wisdom and advice. I've never forgotten her answer to my question about how she got started. She said, "I just hung out my shingle and said, 'Open for business.'" Those words gave me the courage to do just that.

I so appreciated the time and insights she so generously gave me, with no thought of how the favor might be returned. After that lunch we touched base a couple of times a year, and even though I never did find a way to reciprocate her kindnesses, I always held her in my mind as my example of how to give to others. I don't think she ever even knew the impact she had on my career with just that one conversation.

My grandmother had the ability to induce guilt with one phrase, muttered in her heavy Yiddish accent: "Oy, what I do for you," she'd say with a roll of her eyes, implying that she always did more for us than we could ever do for her. This chapter is about adopting exactly the opposite attitude and instead thinking, *What can I do for you?*

One of the strongest ways to increase likability and foster a connection is to demonstrate that we understand someone else's needs and are happy to help fulfill them. By drawing on what we have learned about the other laws of likability, we can apply our creativity to expand the kinds of value we have to offer others, giving to them in ways that speak directly to what might be useful for them.

I'll Scratch Your Back . . .

". . . If you scratch mine" is usually the way that phrase ends. The reality, however, is that there is extraordinary value in doing things for others simply because you want to, not because you expect anything in return. That's the *law of giving*: Do because you can, give first. Giving creates value. It doesn't always mean exerting major effort or making grand gestures. Even by extending yourself in small ways you are sending the signal that you think the other person is worth the effort, and that you want to help.

Sometimes it is easy to see how you may help another person. Other times it's not as obvious, especially with regard to someone who may be more senior than you. But everyone needs and appreciates assistance. Don't underestimate your ability to bring value to someone else.

Several years ago, through a mutual friend, I was introduced to James, a top executive at a company whose customers were high school students. I had an idea for a series of skills workshops for teenagers, and James and I had lunch to discuss whether the workshops would be a good fit with his company's offerings. We agreed fairly quickly that my workshops weren't the right complement for his company, but our conversation was stimulating nonetheless, and we continued discussing business challenges in specific and general ways.

Both financially and professionally, James was significantly more successful than I was, but by listening attentively to what he told me about his work, and exerting some extra effort to follow up, I was able to offer him assistance. I demonstrated the e-blackboard site at the university where I was teaching and sent him book recommendations I thought might be useful. I wanted to show him that I comprehended what he'd told me, had the ability to suggest solutions and resources, and thought his endeavors were worth supporting. Nothing I did was any big deal, but it demonstrated that I valued our discussion and his work.

One of my coaching colleagues, Tanya, has a great story about her transition from the corporate world to establishing her own business as a coach and trainer. She was traveling frequently for business, and as part of that work she often had to hire independent trainers to conduct off-site sessions. After working with and closely observing these contractors numerous times (and paying them top dollar for their services), she realized that she could conduct these sessions just as effectively. And she wanted to give it a shot.

She talked to her boss, and he went out of his way to support her, sending her to educational seminars to develop her skill sets and giving her opportunities to conduct internal training seminars. Her boss still expected Tanya to carry her regular workload too, but he wanted to keep her motivated and happy, and so he determined that if she wanted to acquire these new skills while she was a part of his team, he was going to make sure she did it well. He created a supportive office environment, which let Tanya know he really was behind her.

Tanya eventually did so well with the internal training sessions she conducted, and enjoyed the work so much, that she left the company to establish her own business. Her former boss became one of her biggest clients.

Doing things for others and being generous with your support and your time are likable qualities. They also foster the law of familiarity, keeping you in people's minds and giving them reasons to want to stay in touch with you and continue growing the relationship.

In Chapter 8, I said that there are two things you want to do before you end a conversation: Make the person you are talking to feel good (mood memory), and create the opportunity for follow-up. Extending a helping hand is one of the best ways to follow up, and it also opens the door for continued contact going forward. With every interaction you increase familiarity and similarity. The law of giving is a powerful enhancement of every other law of likability.

Do Unto Others

There are so many ways to provide value to another person, and everyone has something to offer. Whether it's by suggesting resources, creating opportunities for meaningful interactions, or offering feedback and support, we can employ the law of giving by seeking out chances to give back. People tend to respond to situations in the same tried-and-true ways, which works on a certain level: If something has been effective in the past, chances are it will prove so again in the future. But sticking only to these well-tested methods can narrow our view of what we can do for others. Perhaps we feel as if we don't have time to make the extra effort, or we wonder when doing so would be appropriate. By broadening our perspectives and expanding our creative approaches to situations, we can understand that giving is a never-ending process and benefits us throughout the lengths of our careers. By embracing opportunities to help others, we can recognize all the ways, big and small, that giving adds value to our relationships.

Connections

I have always been a matchmaker. As soon as I meet someone, I start thinking about other people I know whom they would want to meet. When I put people together I'm putting all the other laws into action: First, I get curious; then, I focus on listening; and then my synapses start to fire when I recognize similarities. As I'm talking with someone, ideas about whom I might connect that person with jump into my mind. I'll be thinking, "I know someone who used to work at that company," or "I have a friend who attended that coaching program," or "I know someone in your field who also just moved to the area." The points of connection continue unfolding.

Before I introduce people I always ask them if they want to be introduced, since I only want to make the introduction if both people are interested (I'll elaborate on this subject in the section Favors and Advice, later in this chapter). I'm also mindful that introductions are an extension of the person who makes them, and carry the weight of that person's reputation. When I've been introduced to someone because a colleague thinks there'd be an opportunity for connection between me and the other person, I always update the introducer about the progress of the relationship once the introduction has been made. By connecting two people for whatever good reasons, you are applying the laws of familiarity and giving, and creating opportunities for meaningful interactions to take place.

Invitations

Who doesn't like to get invited to a party? Extending an invitation to an event is one of the easiest things you can do for someone. Think about what you have in common—interests, background, people—and then look for opportunities to include that person in events or activities that speak to that commonality.

Inform Others About an Event

Every year, I attend CWIB, the conference I mentioned in the opening story of this chapter. It is one of the best ways I can spend a day. The speakers are engaging; the topics are timely; and the day, quite simply, is fun. But more than anything else, I find the conference inspiring. It is impossible not to be inspired when you are in a roomful of other professionals (hundreds of them) who want to help one another. The attendees are mostly women, but each year there are surprisingly more and more men who have discovered the value of the event, and their enthusiastic attendance further increases the opportunities for forming meaningful connections. Of course I want to share the event with others (including, while I'm at it, the readers of this book—go to www.cwib.org for more information). As soon as the date is announced each year, I send an e-mail to everyone I think would be interested. So far, someone has always joined me, and I am thrilled to be able to introduce people to the value of the conference.

A conference is just one example of an event to which you can extend an invitation. If you belong to a club, group, or organization that allows nonmembers to attend, that is the perfect chance to think about inviting someone to the next gathering. My former colleague Frederick is an adventure junkie who belongs to a club of extreme-sports enthusiasts who arrange trips to do white-water rafting, bungee jumping, and spelunking. When a new hire named Tony joined our team and Frederick discovered that he had similar interests, he immediately forwarded the club link to Tony. It was a simple gesture, but it presented Tony with new opportunities for doing things he loved, made him feel welcomed to our team, and showed that Frederick was friendly and inclusive, which quickly established a basis for strong collegial communication and trust between them.

There are any number of events that can provide opportunities for further contact and continued connection. I always appreciate hearing about webinars or lectures that pertain to my work. I often invite other people to participate in a volunteer activity I'm doing if I think it would interest them. And right after I'd moved to a new town, I was pretty excited to get invited to a women's night out. It was a fun and completely casual event that offered the chance to form all kinds of new connections.

The events you inform people of don't even have to be ones you are attending; they can simply be things that crossed your path and that you thought the person might be interested in. Don't flood people's inboxes, of course, and don't invite everyone you know to everything you hear about. Make it personal. This shows people that you're thinking specifically of them.

Create a Group

When I attended CWIB for the first time in the early 2000s, I was still transitioning from my finance life into my current career. I was incredibly motivated by meeting so many women who were either already established in my new field, in the early stages of transitioning into it (like I was), or somewhere in between. I even suggested we start an informal peer-mentoring group to help each other out. And so I e-mailed four of the women I met about the idea, set a date, and then almost called it off when only two of them could make it.

Looking back, I am so glad I didn't call it off. There were just three of us at the first meeting, sitting in the café at a bookstore with no agenda. We simply shared what we were working on. A month or two later, I tried again to get our original group of five together. This time everyone could make it, and we all felt energized by the gathering. We began meeting regularly. As I started connecting with more and more people in my new field, I expanded the invite list to our get-togethers. Finally we moved from the bookstore to my apartment for our first "official" meeting. More than a dozen women attended. I had formed a group.

Over time the group got so large that the location changed again. We established a Yahoo group so that we could share our resources, events, books, and contact information collectively online. We now use LinkedIn for this purpose, and there are more than fifty women who participate. Each member was personally invited to join our network by someone who already belonged, and our informal association has become a tremendous way to support and help one another.

Groups can be formed around any shared interest, professional or personal. Book clubs, investment clubs, and poker nights are all great excuses for connecting with people who have shared interests and inviting others to join you in forming the connections.

Create an Event

One of my colleagues, Larry, organizes a monthly lunch to which he invites a rotating group of core business associates. Everyone pays for themselves, and Larry arranges a set menu with the restaurant so that costs are reasonable and anticipated. The lunches are always an excellent chance to connect with new people in your field, catch up with acquaintances, and think creatively about possible collaborations or resource sharing.

The industry lunch is just one example of ways to include people in a shared event. Think about what would interest people in your network, and plan a way to connect them through an activity. Organize a cooking lesson by a local chef; invite a financial planner you know to hold a seminar. The event doesn't have to cost you anything beyond a little time and effort, and the rewards will be countless.

My neighbor Bonnie, a former PTA president and mom of a high school junior, approached the superintendent of our local school system about creating a college prep curriculum. Budget cuts meant that new programs couldn't be funded, so Bonnie responded by creating a workshop at her home for students to prepare for college interviews. She contacted parents to arrange for a group of students to gather at her house, and invited me over to lead the workshop. The event sparked many productive discussions afterward, and the students acquired valuable skills, and in the end, it generated such interest that the parents sought to expand the program.

Information and Articles

Marge was the head of training at a high-profile museum. We were introduced through a mutual friend, and commonalities between us were not immediately obvious: She was much older than I was, had spent her career in a field that I didn't know much about, and had something of a reticent demeanor, tending not to share too much personal information in conversations and keeping everything strictly professional.

Right before I was about to conduct a team-building seminar at the museum, I received news that my son had a serious medical condition. I suppose that Marge picked up on something in my voice or my body language, because she asked me if I was all right. I was so overwhelmed by the news that I didn't even realize the extent to which I was explaining my distress; I just poured it all out. I was so grateful that someone was there, offering to listen.

I had no idea that my personal disclosure would lead to her making one of her own. It turned out that Marge's son had a serious medical condition as well, so grave that at age 15 he was completely dependent on others for everything and lived with full-time care. Wow. Her story stopped me in my tracks. She said that she wasn't telling me this to make me feel better or worse, but just to let me know that she understood. She had been dealing with her son's extremely difficult medical issues for years.

Her openness steadied me, and I was able to refocus on the seminar and solidly deliver, but even more important was what came afterward. Marge began sending me articles and information to help me navigate the challenges my family and I were now dealing with. As I learned more about her situation, I began thinking of ways I could be of help to her. We shared strategies, relevant news stories, and medical updates. There was true reciprocity between us, born out of care and understanding. At some point we both realized that we had become trusted, valued friends, and though we continue to work together it is not just about the work anymore, it's about the relationship, the friendship. And as I always say, I want to work with people I'm friends with. And that's where I am with Marge.

Somewhere during a conversation, you are likely going to hear about something that truly interests the other person. When following up with people afterward, you have the perfect opportunity for forwarding links or information they might find engaging. Even if no ideas come to you during the conversation, make a note on the back of their business card or next to their name in your BlackBerry about what their interests are. This allows you to tuck away the information until you do hear about something that would be of interest to them or, if you want to be more proactive, to put a little effort into finding something that may be helpful, which may be as simple as an online article or the names of some books. Take five minutes to query your network for opinions or resources that the person might find useful.

A word of caution, which is largely common sense but bears mentioning: Understand your audience. What one person finds valuable may be another person's spam. Only forward information and links that speak to the person's genuine interests.

Favors and Advice

For many people, favors are difficult to request but easy to grant. The same can be true of advice: We consult people we admire, but underplay the wisdom and insights we have to pass on to someone else. We all have knowledge, skills, experience, and unique perspectives to contribute. Sharing these things extends the circles of context for connecting among our networks and gives us opportunities to deepen our relationships with others. Even if you are just starting out in your career, you have valuable perspectives and advice to share. Older colleagues are often curious about the outlook of younger generations, and they could be eager to hear your views.

Here are examples of some of the favors I've recently done for others. At the bottom of the list, fill in at least three things you did or can do for other people. Think about your life and your associations, and add three more ideas for giving advice or doing a favor.

- Sent a PR lead to a colleague
- Answered questions related to my area of expertise
- Gave advice to colleagues about pricing their services
- Referred a potential client to a friend

- Talked to interested colleagues about the finance profession, training profession, and entrepreneurship
- Talked to my friends' children about the universities I attended and at which I teach
- Gave away the clothes, toys, and books that my kids have outgrown
- Invited someone to join me at an invitation-only event
- _____
- _____
- _____

Favors and advice are things you should offer freely, but conscientiously. A favor is only a favor when someone wants it. And stay aware of when the circle of favors is such that your favor for someone else involves a favor to you. This happens frequently when introducing people to one another. Whenever I meet someone curious about transitioning into hedge funds, I reach out to my friend Darrell, who has been in that field for his whole career. Darrell is always happy to speak with anyone I put him in touch with, but he does it as a favor to me more than anything else.

Make the effort to connect people with the information and resources you have at your disposal, but stay mindful of how you do it. Don't wear out your welcome by introducing too many people to the same desirable contact. The point is to truly add value, not take advantage of someone else's goodwill.

Likewise, if advice is given without sensitivity, it can come off as someone being nosy or trying to tell you what to do. When my friend Sally was hired by the employer of another one of our friends, Fran, the two of them ran into trouble in the office even though they'd been friends for a while. During Sally's first week on the job, Fran was full of advice for her about how to acclimate, pointing out which colleagues were irritating, which ones were good team players, and so on. Fran was only trying to help, but Sally felt as if she'd immediately been restricted in terms of how she could behave in the office and whom she could interact with. If she formed a connection with someone Fran didn't particularly care for, she felt as if she was being disloyal to Fran. Things between them got tense. It took some time for them to grow comfortable working together and get their friendship back on track.

The lesson here: When in doubt, *ask permission*. Simply inquire whether the other person wants to hear your advice by saying something such as, "Are you interested in an opinion, or is now not the right time?" or "Do you want my advice, or do you just need to get this off your chest?"

LIVE THE LAW: *WHAT CAN I DO FOR YOU?*

Create an action plan for following the law of giving. Based on the previous sections, mark down specifically *what* you will do, *who* you will do it for, and *when* you will get it done. Write down at least one thing you will do in each category, and choose a different person for each planned action. Then do it.

ACTION PLAN

CONNECTION

WHO _____ TO WHOM _____

WHY _____ WHEN _____

INVITATION

TO WHAT _____

WHO _____ WHEN _____

INFORMATION OR ARTICLE

WHAT _____

WHO _____ WHEN _____

FAVOR OR ADVICE

WHAT _____

WHO _____ WHEN _____

What Goes Around, Comes Around

When you give freely to others, not only do you increase your
likability and aid other people, you almost always get something
unintended in return. I am an avid traveler and my conversations
with people often come around to the subject of favorite vacation
spots and destinations. If someone is headed to a place I've explored, I always offer to share my experiences. When I follow up
with people after one of these conversations, I'll frequently reference a resort they mentioned or forward links to places I think
they might like to visit. Sometimes I even send along a few reviews
I've uncovered. This stokes my own thirst for exploring new
places.

During one of my conversations with James, the top executive,
he once mentioned to me some technical issues he was facing with
a project under development. I am definitely not a techie, but my
husband definitely is. I called up Mike, explained what James was
trying to accomplish, and learned about the options. Then it was
my pleasure to share those insights with James. Not only was I
able to save him some effort and pass along useful knowledge, I
also got educated during the process. It was a win-win experience.

And then there are the times when, because of ways you've

willingly given in the past, you find yourself unexpectedly on the receiving end. More than a year after I met James, we once again had an opportunity to talk. This time I was explaining to him a business idea of mine. More than anything else, it was a chance for me to hear myself flesh out the idea to an astute businessman. James replied that when I was ready to pursue the idea, he would happily help. I didn't expect this gracious offer, and was deeply touched by it, but that is part of what is behind the law of giving: When you simply do something for other people out of a genuine desire to help them, more often than not they are going to want to reciprocate. Giving inspires giving. The result is mutual growth and a stronger relationship.

Be honest with yourself about your intentions. If you do have expectations that you will be repaid for your efforts, that's not the same as giving freely, so don't try to disguise it as such. Your motivations will be detected at some level by the other person. To truly harness the law of giving—and its rewards—you have to genuinely feel that you don't expect anything in return.

Pay It Forward

This chapter opened with a story about Amy, who is an example to me of what it means to give to someone else, without expectations. I remember that when I got together with Amy, I paid for lunch. It seemed like the least I could do since she had shared her insights and experiences with me so generously, and I had gathered hoards of knowledge from the conversation. I remember feeling as if I could never repay her for all the wisdom she so graciously bestowed, and to be honest, I still feel that way.

What I have done to try to repay her kindness and generosity in some way is to emulate her giving. At every possible chance, I pay it forward. When someone asks me for a favor, some advice, or some of my time, I almost unequivocally answer, "Yes." I give willingly and in as much abundance as I can. Amy put me on this path of generosity and taught me that "what you give is what you get." Even when it seems as if we are not getting anything in return for our efforts, patience can help us understand how the things we do positively impact ours and other people's lives in many different ways. That law of patience is what we will explore in Chapter 11.

Refresh Your Memory

The Law of Giving: Give First. Do because you can, and because giving creates value.

Do Unto Others. There are countless ways to give freely to others, including making introductions to other people they might benefit from knowing, extending invitations to events and activities, sharing resources, doing favors, and giving advice.

You Can Help. Be proactive about determining how you can help the people in your circle. Set the law of giving in motion by creating an action plan detailing *what* you are going to do, *who* you will do it for, and *when* you will do it. Then do it.

What Goes Around, Comes Around. You may not always be the explicit recipient of the law of giving, but when you give to others, more often than not you reap rewards in return.

Pay It Forward. Repay kindnesses and generosity bestowed upon you by continuing the giving. Extend yourself freely to others to sustain the positive cycle of giving.

11

The Law of Patience

"A man who is a master of patience is master of everything else."
—George Savile, seventeenth-century statesman

M ore than a year ago, I received an e-mail from Aaron, the director of learning and development initiatives at a media company. He was looking for someone to conduct a series of training seminars, and one of my former NYU students had recommended me to him. After briefing me on what he wanted, I put together a proposal and sent it to him. Then his agenda changed. We brainstormed more possibilities and I prepared another proposal, but the department still wasn't ready to green-light the program. I continued checking in with him from time to time and told him to consider me a resource, which he did. He reached out to me frequently with questions about training companies, other independent trainers, topics, pricing, and industry resources. I provided him with suggestions and recommended training companies that covered topics my business, Executive Essentials, did not. Every time he had a thought for a new training direction, I was on his list of people to get a proposal from.

After drafting my third proposal for services and still not

signing a contract, I was at the point where many people would have written off the client. To be honest, I really didn't think Aaron's company would ever become one of my clients. But that didn't stop me from quickly responding to his questions. With patience, no expectations, and a continued desire to build the relationship and help as I could, I became his go-to person in many situations. Once he queried me about a vendor he was vetting, but I wasn't familiar with this business, so I sent out the vendor name to my network and shared with him the feedback I received.

Six proposals and more than twelve months later, I got another proposal request from him. And this time I landed the job. In this case, the seventh time was the charm.

They say that patience is a virtue. This might be naturally true for some people, but it certainly isn't true for me. Being patient is difficult for me, but it also yields incredible value. The benefits of patience come back to you in so many ways. That is why the subject of patience is the culminating chapter of this book.

Some of you reading the story about Aaron may have been thinking, "Forget it, I would have given up on that potential client long ago; life is too short to put forth so much effort for free." And it would have seemed reasonable, given the situation, to discontinue the relationship and cut my losses. If I had, though, I never would have landed a client with whom I now work regularly.

In the end, you have to do what feels right for you. I am not a Pollyanna who believes that everyone is nice and has good intentions, but I do believe that most people have good intentions, and I choose to believe the best about people until they give me reasons not to. As you read this chapter, leave behind any tendencies toward impatience, jumping to conclusions, or assuming negative interpretations of a situation, even if only for the duration of the chapter. It is often easier to shut down or turn away and give in to impatience because it requires less effort than being patient, but it can be a self-fulfilling prophecy, and you may limit yourself as a result.

Give It Time, Things Happen

Early on in life I learned the saying "quid pro quo"—one thing in return for another—and for the first part of my career I tried to live by that guideline. If someone did something for me, I understood there was an expectation that the favor would be returned. I thought I was living by a standard of equality, and it not only made sense to me, it seemed fair. It took me a while to realize that not everyone lived by this code of fairness. I found myself wondering when my good deeds and kind gestures would be returned.

I remember one colleague, Todd, who had asked for a few favors when we first started working together, and I'd happily done them. Soon, though, I realized that it was a one-way street with him. I started feeling annoyed by him, and treating him with a bit of an attitude. I even started to avoid him because I got tense whenever I was around him. He had no idea why I was acting that way toward him, and at the time I wasn't self-aware enough to recognize the reasons for my behavior, either.

When I think back on the situation now, I can see that I felt slighted, and interpreted his lack of reciprocity as him taking advantage of me. My impatience and my expectations got in the way, and our work relationship deteriorated. During my exit interview with that company, I learned that Todd had given his manager a glowing recommendation about me. Knowing that I wanted to work on a project involving his manager's client, Todd put in a good word for me—I just never knew. I wonder what may have been different in my career and in my relationship with Todd if I hadn't constantly been thinking, "Where's mine?"

What I have learned is to let go of expectations. I don't mean to say that "if you don't have expectations, you can't be disappointed." Not at all. Getting rid of expectations isn't about flattening your experience so that you are never disappointed; rather, it's about freeing your mind of the burden of waiting for the expectations to be fulfilled. You have enough to think about, so take expectations off your list. Patience produces results. This is the essence of the *law of patience*: Give it time, things happen. Your results may not be exactly *what* you expect, and they may not happen *when* you expect them. In fact, you may not even be aware of the results at all, as I learned with Todd.

It Comes Back to You

I could have called this chapter "What Goes Around, Comes Around," because I believe that if you act selflessly in your relationships, if you make it about the other person and not about yourself, good things will come of those actions. Sometimes the fruits of your interactions appear quickly, as when a conversation turns into a contact that turns into a job. Other times a benefit may show up unexpectedly, years in the future. And to be honest, sometimes nothing at all happens, and that's all right, too.

In Chapter 9, I told you about Mark. He's a master at keeping his name in people's minds. He regularly holds intimate luncheons at which a diverse array of people mix, including many journalists and media professionals. The lunches are one of Mark's ways of giving back: By connecting all these people who have been important in his professional journey, he creates opportunities for them to build meaningful working relationships with one another. And he found that soon after he started hosting the lunches, not only did the people in his professional circle start forming strong connections with one another, but the impact of the connections had a rippling effect. Even he was on the receiving end one time when a reporter he didn't already know called with an interview request. It seems that Mark had been pointed out to this reporter by one of his media colleagues.

Here's one of my favorite examples of how "it comes back to you" has played out in my life. It's a story about my colleague Randi, whom I met five years ago while coaching students at NYU. She was a coach, too, and had a great energy. We exchanged our background information, and when Randi learned about one particular project I was working on, she quite boldly asked if I would help her get in touch with that client. I must admit I was a little surprised at her forwardness, but I kept in mind my rules: Always have the conversation, stay open and curious, and do because you can. I am always eager to help, but I am also careful to ensure that when I make an introduction it's beneficial to both parties. Introductions are an extension of your reputation. By introducing someone, you are extending your confidence in the person as being worth knowing. Since I didn't really know Randi yet, I wasn't sure how I felt about connecting her with one of my contacts so quickly. I responded, "I'm happy to talk more and get to know you and see how I might be able to help."

Soon after that Randi and I had lunch, and I learned that she had actually done work for the client in the past, but had lost her contacts because of turnover at the company. At the end of lunch I said to her, "Since I've never seen your work, I am not able to give a testimonial about it, but here's what I can do. I'm happy to connect you with the right person, let them know you have done work for them in the past, fill them in about how you and I know one another, and then you can take it from there." Randi seemed completely happy with the suggestion.

After that, she regularly e-mailed me with updates about her communication with the client, and we continued to get to know each other. I invited her to join the networking group I'd founded and she became an active participant. At one of the meetings she ran over to me, eager to thank me. "For what?" I asked her, utterly confused. She told me excitedly that the client had just hired her for a large project. Even though I had only had a small hand in the accomplishment, she attributed it fully to me. I was of course thrilled that it had worked out for her, and then didn't really give it another thought.

Four years later I was putting together a program on an extremely tight deadline and needed some quick help with the material. I put out a frantic call to the members of my networking group, which Randi was still a part of. Randi replied to my call for help within minutes. She knew a lot about the topic and was even willing to rearrange her schedule to talk with me. She sent me a bunch of articles, brought me a book when we met, and gave me a ton of good advice. It was a fifteen-minute conversation over coffee, and I got hours of value out of it. And that's the law of patience in action. I never said, hinted, or even thought "You owe me" when I'd put Randi in touch with the client all those years ago, and I don't think that at the time she thought, "I owe her." But when she could give, she did.

I have countless stories about how the law of giving has given back to me over time. Perhaps one of the most striking was when I was contacted by a man named Zeke who worked at a hedge fund and was looking for someone to conduct training sessions for the fund's directors. When I asked him who had referred him to me, he revealed that he had actually gotten my name from an HR forum and couldn't remember the name of the person who posted the comment. We went on to do a huge amount of work together. To this day, I have no idea whom to thank for getting me one of my largest clients ever. I did know whom to thank when I got calls from the Metropolitan Museum of Art and Jazz at Lincoln Center. It turned out that Marge, the woman with whom I'd worked at another high-profile museum, and with whom I'd bonded because of our sons' medical conditions, had recommended me immediately when training colleagues at these two cultural institutions asked her for recommendations—even though I'd never asked her for references or leads.

The law of patience is never far from my mind. You never know when things will happen, but with patience they *do* happen.

Or It Goes to Someone Else

If there is still a part of you that can't let go of the quid pro quo concept, think of the law of patience as an extension of the "pay it forward" idea. Sometimes, your giving is repaid not to you but passed on to someone else. You do something for someone, and the recipient of your kindness in turn shows a kindness to someone else.

I am still awestruck by the generosity of Amy, the woman who gave me so much wisdom about launching my business after I met her at the Columbia Women in Business conference. We didn't even have that much follow-up contact after our initial meeting—a very productive lunch and some phone calls and e-mails now and again—but her willingness to help me so freely had a powerful effect on me. For years afterward I channeled that spirit, giving back to other entrepreneurs who were just starting out. I spoke to student-entrepreneur groups at universities, arranged for phone conversations, and probably met with more than 100 people over the course of five years. Amy never knew that she was the one who inspired me to give in this way, and she had no expectations that her generosity would be repaid.

Amy was the first of many people who so willingly gave their time to advise me, assist me, and teach me as I was growing my business. Their generous gifts have rebounded to the benefit of others as I have consistently given my time, advice, and assistance to those around me. You may not know how your giving has inspired or positively influenced others, but have faith. The goodness you put out in the world multiplies.

You'll Get Your Chance

Even though I was profoundly influenced by Amy's generous spirit, I didn't think I'd ever get the chance to repay her directly for all that she'd done for me. Yet I had been thinking about her a lot as I was writing the final section of the book when, completely out of the blue one day, I ran into her! I couldn't believe it. I was sitting at a café with a friend when a woman I didn't immediately recognize stopped by the table to say hello to my friend. When my friend introduced us, we quickly figured out how we already knew each other.

It was poetic running into her—this woman who had unwittingly played such a pivotal role in my career—at that precise moment. "I just wrote about you!" I blurted out excitedly. When Amy looked at me in confusion, I explained the law of giving to her. She matter-of-factly stated that she had the exact same attitude about giving, and threw up her hands in a "whatever happens" gesture, explaining that she did things without ever expecting that she would get anything in return.

Even after our other friend left, Amy and I continued chatting like childhood friends for more than an hour. We picked up right where we'd left off, trying to catch up on the dozens of things that had been going on in each of our lives. She told me that she had just applied for a job. It happened to be with an organization that I'd worked with for years. Finally, *finally*, there was something I could do for her. We set up a lunch date to discuss all the ways we might help each other and even work together.

As soon as I got home I called the director of the organization to learn more about the position Amy was applying for, and then I submitted a written recommendation of her. I also sent her a link to other open positions she was qualified for at the organization.

Once you start fully living the law of giving, you will find that you are eager to do kindnesses for people who do them for you. But the law of patience isn't just about trusting that the good things you do will positively impact you or others; it's about trusting that you will have the chance to give back for the generosity you've been shown. When you can't yet give back directly for help you've received, pay it forward. And trust that you may well get your chance to directly help the people who have selflessly helped you.

When you can't give back right away, sometimes the opportunity you do eventually receive to give back is even bigger and better than you may have thought possible. Since reconnecting with Amy, I've been able to make introductions for her and give her references that have helped her land work with two major organizations. I have also been able to mentor her (though I can hardly believe it!) about pricing and client selection.

Be patient. The ways you can give may not be immediately obvious, but you will get your chance.

Friendships Grow in Time

Throughout this book we've looked at building relationships. The truth of it is that you won't want to build relationships with every single person you meet, and that is okay. There's no need to burn bridges with those people. You can simply choose not to pursue the relationships. But remember too that friendships can take time to grow.

We all have that childhood friend we love, but we know that if we met that person for the first time today we probably wouldn't be friends. This plays itself out in our adult lives too, and we need to remember that sometimes it pays to be patient.

For me, my relationship with my sister, April, is one of the strongest examples of the principle that friendships grow with time. Even though we're siblings, we couldn't be more different. She has tremendous innate skill as a designer, putting together colors, textures, materials, and patterns, and she has singlehandedly redesigned entire rooms in her house, to stunning effect. I have none of these gifts, and when I was decorating my own house I relied on her expertise every step of the way. I excel at more traditionally academic, less artistic fields, so when April is sending a critical communication, she runs it by me first for feedback on language, content, messaging, and tone. She tends to be a bit messy. I'm meticulously organized. She loves and follows fashion, which I've never had a strong passion for. I love adventure, scary rides, and roughing it—three things that she more than happily lives without. Our natural skills and abilities are diametrically opposite in almost every instance, and yet she unfailingly knows what and how I think almost as well as I do, and we constantly rely on one another's unique strengths and gifts.

Time and shared experiences are key ingredients to creating bonds that last. I first met Gabby when I was still working on Wall Street. We were introduced by a mutual friend who thought we would click. We'd both gone to the same business school, and we were building our own businesses in the same field. With all that to talk about, I anticipated becoming fast friends.

She came to my office for an hour-long conversation, but when she left I felt oddly let down. Nothing clicked. There was no bonding as if we'd known one another forever because of all our similarities. Our talk was interesting, but I was left feeling neutral. I hadn't yet learned to let go of my expectations around people as well.

Since there was so much overlap in our interests and potential for collaboration, we planned a follow-up meeting. It was on my way to this second appointment that my mother's advice to me as a teenager came to mind. She used to say, "Give a guy three dates. If the first one isn't going well, you are having a bad day. If the second one isn't going well, he is having a bad day. If the third date doesn't go well, then you know you gave it a chance."

After the second meeting with Gabby I still saw the professional potential in our relationship but didn't think about it much beyond that. We continued pursuing some common projects, and almost imperceptibly began to blur the line between business and friendship. I don't know how many times Gabby and I got together before I started to think of her as a friend. Certainly it was more than my mother's magic "three." But she is now one of my most valued friends, and has been for years. If I hadn't been patient and remained open to the possibility that our relationship could grow, I would have missed out not only on a great business associate but also a wonderful friend.

I also would have missed out on a valuable lesson about building solid relationships with people who are different from me. Sometimes those can wind up being the strongest bonds, since we have to give them the time and room to develop. For all the outward similarities Gabby and I had, it turned out that we had quite different styles. She is an introvert with quiet confidence; when she thinks, she does it in silence. I am an extrovert and a processor, and I think about something by talking through it out loud. While getting to know Gabby, I had to adjust my style so that I didn't come on too strong or push for a closeness that neither of us were authentically feeling right off the bat.

When you are impatient with a relationship, your actions can be read as pushy or needy—not exactly likable qualities. Truly lasting friendships are rarely instantaneous. Give them time and room to grow. Now when I meet someone new, I look for the ways we may connect and the things we might build a relationship on, and I find humor in what makes us different. Having acquaintances is great, but I always remind myself that they might turn into relationships somewhere down the road. Stay open to the possibilities inherent in connection, and always have the conversation.

Be Patient

As I was writing this book I attended a conference and ran into Cheryl, another colleague of mine. We regularly cross paths, but this time, as we were talking with a few other people, she said, "Michelle is a terrific networker." Then she looked at me and asked, "It comes back to you, right?" I looked at her curiously, thinking about the question, and said, "It goes somewhere. I don't really keep track. Sometimes, if you give to someone, they give to someone else, and that's fine with me. I am happy as long as it keeps going. I don't keep a scorecard."

Patience is the culminating chapter of this book because it's needed to embrace the other laws. We must have patience with ourselves and with others—patience to find the similarities, build the relationship, establish trust, and create familiarity. Having patience means choosing to do something without expecting to get something back. It means doing it because you can and because you want to. Being patient means knowing and trusting that somewhere in the universe, some person or some good cause is benefiting from the way you have lived the laws of likability.

Refresh Your Memory

The Law of Patience. Give it time, things happen.

It Comes Back to You, or It Goes Somewhere Else. You may not know what the results of your generous actions will be, or whether you will ever directly benefit from them. That's okay. Kindness repays kindness, even if it's not in obvious ways.

You'll Get Your Chance. Be patient with yourself. You never know *how* or *when* you may be able to bring value to someone else.

Friendships Grow in Time. Stay open to the possibility that a relationship may evolve over time. Have patience.

Conclusion: Putting the Book into Action

Likability is more than a nice idea, or a concept of which you should stay mindful—it is an approach to your life and the people in it. The point isn't for you to like everyone and for everyone to like you. Instead, the point is to create meaningful connections that strengthen your relationships, your self-awareness, your productivity, and inevitably, your results. Be authentic in your interactions, and follow the paths of what you truly want to do, not what you think you should do.

Although the abiding principle is set out in law number one—the law of authenticity—the book is not meant to be linear. All the laws of likability are intertwined and work in concert with one another. Based on where you are in your career and how you want to enhance your relationships, you can focus in on the laws that will be most useful for you at this point in time. Choose one and work on incorporating it into your interactions with other people. Once it has become second nature, choose a new law to focus on. Apply the laws with openness and authenticity in mind, and you will become more connected.

People ask me all the time, "How do you get your clients, and how do you build your business?" This book is my attempt to answer those questions. I never knew quite how to explain it until I began to fully understand the value of likability. I used to think that "likability" was something nice but nothing that needed to be taken too seriously. But after that one fateful day in my NYU classroom, I realized that likability is the key to the whole process of developing meaningful relationships. It is the essential bedrock upon which everything else is built.

My business has grown because I "live the book." I go out of my way to provide value beyond the work I am hired to do, without expecting that I will get anything in return. I find that I get repeat business from the clients with whom I have built the strongest relationships, and those relationships have been able to grow because we've found commonalities, we've been proactive about staying in touch and therefore staying in one another's minds, and we talk about things other than work. We simply like each other. And people do business with people they like.

Notes

2: THE LAW OF SELF-IMAGE

1. Daniel Gould, Kenneth Hodge, Kirsten Peterson, and John Giannini, "An Exploratory Examination of Strategies Used by Elite Coaches to Enhance Self-Efficacy in Athletes," *Journal of Sport & Exercise Psychology* 11, no. 2 (June 1989).
2. Joan A. Finn, "Competitive Excellence: It's a Matter of Mind and Body," *The Physician and Sports Medicine* 13, no. 2 (February 1985).

3: THE LAW OF PERCEPTION

1. Based on the internationally acclaimed NBI™ battery of 4- and 8-dimensional instruments.
2. Albert Mehrabian, *Silent Messages* (Belmont, CA: Wadsworth Publishing, 1981), pp. 75–80.

8: THE LAW OF MOOD MEMORY

1. Eric Eich, Dawn Macaulay, and Lee Ryan, "Mood Dependent Memory for Events of the Personal Past," *Journal of Experimental Psychology* 123, no. 2 (June 1994), pp. 201–215.

2. K. A. Nichols and B. G. Champness discuss eye contact and endorphins in "Eye Gaze and GSR," *Journal of Experimental Social Psychology* 7, no. 6 (November 1971), pp. 623–626; and Matthias J. Wieser, Paul Pauli, Georg W. Alpers, and Andreas Mühlberger talk about the heart beating faster because of eye contact in "Is Eye to Eye Contact Really Threatening and Avoided in Social Anxiety?" *Journal of Anxiety Disorders* 23, no. 1 (January 2009), pp. 93–103.

9: THE LAW OF FAMILIARITY

1. "41.6% of the U.S. Population Has a Facebook Account," Social Media Today, http://socialmediatoday.com/index.php?q=-roywells 1/158020/416-us-population-has-facebook-account.
2. Heather Dougherty, "Facebook Reaches Top Ranking in U.S.," Hitwise (blog), March 15, 2010, http://weblogs.hitwise.com/heatherdougherty/2010/03/facebook_reaches_top_ranking_i .html.

Index